DECODING MITHYA

In the Silence, We Find Our Voice:
Decoding the Myths of Womanhood

DR SMITA KAMAT GHOSH

INDIA • SINGAPORE • MALAYSIA

ISBN

Hardcase 979-8-89588-983-1
Paperback 979-8-89556-971-9

Contents

Acknowledgement

Having an idea and turning it into a book is harder than I thought and more rewarding than I could have ever imagined. The experience has been both internally challenging and profoundly fulfilling.

None of this would have been possible without the unwavering support and encouragement from my family. I am deeply grateful to my daughter, Poorna, whose belief in me inspired many of the thoughts behind this book, and my son, who shares in the vision and meaning of this work. My heartfelt thanks also go to my mother, whose wisdom has always guided me, and my father, who has been my constant source of encouragement.

I want to thank my friends, mentors, and guides who helped make this dream a reality. And last, but certainly not least, my deepest gratitude goes to my family, who gave me the freedom and space to think, create, and bring this vision to life.

To everyone who motivated me and believed in me—thank you for helping me achieve my dream.

Foreword

Pre-launch Review

When I first heard about Smita Ghosh's *Decoding Mithya*, my sceptical self only had one thought: another gender-bashing effort. But despite myself, I found myself drawn to Sakhi and her appropriate interactions. It felt like I could be talking to a friend.

I appreciated the general approach - novel indeed.

Gender grouping for pink and blue is an unconscious bias steeped in Western social stereotypes but ingrained in the English-speaking peoples, including us.

If *Decoding Mithya* will give us an equitable world with no gender discrimination for females or males, count me in.

    – *Elizabeth Koshy* Director – Chaitanya School, Ahmedabad

Decoding Mithya inspires a profound vision of a world where men and women stand on truly equal footing, breaking free from the confines of traditional roles and allowing outdated stereotypes to fade into the annals of history. The novel delves deep into the fabric of societal norms, challenging the long-held beliefs that have dictated gender roles for generations. It illuminates the arbitrary nature of these conventions, revealing how they limit personal growth and hinder the collective progress of society.

By presenting characters who defy conventional expectations, the story encourages readers to envision a society where attributes and opportunities are not assigned based on gender but are accessible to all. It underscores the importance of shedding labels like "masculine" and "feminine," promoting instead a unisexual identity where individuality is celebrated without prejudice.

This compelling narrative serves as a clarion call to dismantle the barriers that have historically separated us, advocating for a unified community built on respect, understanding, and equality. The transformative journey depicted in the book is not just a fictional aspiration but a tangible goal that resonates deeply with the pressing need for social evolution in our times. I am wholeheartedly on board with this vision, embracing the challenge to contribute to a world free from discrimination—a world where every person has the freedom to define themselves and their destiny without the constraints of outdated stereotypes.

– Founder CI360/Marketing Consultant

Thanks for sharing the preface and outline of *Decoding Mithya!* The voice is friendly but firm, coming alongside to coax but also to rattle. Sakhi serves as a very personable and insightful narrator through the land of myths, sounding almost like an experienced friend on these stories.

The themes you have decided upon — pink stereotyping, gendered toys, financial illiteracy — are strong and spot-on. When introspective questions are blessed with real stories and combined with activities to offer a blend which fills you up from the insides, the book becomes a space where reading is akin to engaging in an interactive experience that calls for individual growth and that of society at large.

This is a structure that works well, and I'm a fan of the combination of narrative with action. But the book also offers solutions on how we can stop it. I feel that readers will relate so well to the issues *Decoding Mithya* deals with that they would be urged from deep within them to question many myths passed down as tradition.

Best regards,

– ***Venkat K. Naidu*** Head Media Sales, Value Research India Private Limited

Decoding Mithya is an interesting book by Dr. Smita Ghosh where she has tried to debunk 5 widely prevalent myths which gave shape to the perceptions about womanhood. While each chapter is a break across stereotypes such as "pink for girls," and "misogyny & menstruation," it is supported by stories, real-life examples, and research that break the norms prevalent across society. The friendly guide in this journey is Sakhi, a character more real than those of today. The preface reads as an apicum that sets the tone for reflection into how seemingly small things such as colour preferences can install strong grooves in gender roles, but wield strong effects on women's lives. Generally, this makes a tremendous call for inclusiveness and unabated tackling of outdated gender stereotypes.

– *Dhwani Gadhvi,* Student, Rashtriya Raksha University

Gender discrimination, though a persistent issue in modern society, has roots that stretch back through history. Yet, wisdom from ancient texts like the Bhagavad Gita offers profound insights that challenge these inequalities. In this book, Smita, a dear friend, beautifully unravels the myths surrounding gender bias, revealing how the Gita transcends superficial divisions and speaks to the equality of all beings at the level of the soul. By exploring timeless teachings and their relevance to today's world, Smita hopes to foster a deeper understanding of true equality, where wisdom triumphs over prejudice.

Looking forward with great excitement to this insightful read!

– *Sonal Narang,* Vice Principal, Anand Niketan Satellite Campus, Ahmedabad

The Preface of Dr. Smita's upcoming book *Decoding Mithya* serves as an intriguing entry point, offering insight into her motivation and intention. This book will surely shed light on how deeply ingrained stereotypes shape our identities and experiences. The preface invites readers to challenge our preconceived notions. The opening is engaging and prepares readers for a curious journey ahead....

A compelling start!

Hope your book sparks important conversations and brings in the much-needed positive change.

All the best, Smita.

*– **Rakesh Mundye,*** Principal Graphic Designer
Times of India, Goa

From where I stand as her daughter, my mother's book delves deeply into the stereotypes that shape how women are perceived and treated. Through the lens of Sakhi, she shatters myths like pink stereotyping, gendered toys, and the taboos surrounding menstruation and financial literacy. These are challenges I have faced firsthand, and her powerful message has become a strong call to break out of these confining roles. Her exploration of these 'Mithyas' is both personal and relatable, paving the way for me to challenge and change these narratives. She has truly been a source of inspiration and pride for me.

*– **Poorna Ghosh***

Being the son of my mother, a woman of profound values, I am deeply grateful and proud to carry the principles she has instilled within me. This book delves into the destructive and unfounded beliefs surrounding gender roles and the rigid traits society imposes upon men and women. I stand proud, both as her son and as someone deeply moved and enlightened by the profound words within these pages.

*– **Ujaan Ghosh***

(This message from Poorna and Ujaan, my beloved children, holds a special place in my heart. Their words not only express their thoughts but also embody the spirit and values we cherish as a family. I am incredibly proud of the individuals they are becoming, and their contributions inspire me daily as we navigate this journey together.)

Preface

From the very first words I penned for this book, I knew it would be more than just a story; it would be a reflection of the experiences, emotions, and questions that have shaped my journey. Writing this book has been an incredibly personal process, allowing me to explore themes that have long resonated with me—love, loss, identity, and the complexities of human connection.

As an author, I believe in the transformative power of storytelling to shed light on our shared experiences. Through the characters and their challenges, I aimed to explore not only their individual paths but also the universal struggles we all face. While the world depicted in these pages is grounded in reality, the emotions and conflicts are deeply authentic, shaped by my observations, interactions, and the lasting impressions they have left on me.

This book was born from a deep desire to give voice to the silent struggles, the unspoken words, and the quiet victories we all endure. My hope is that within these pages, readers will not only find an engaging narrative but also pieces of themselves—familiar emotions, thoughts, or reflections that resonate with their own journeys.

In a world where stereotypes often shape perceptions and dictate opportunities, this book stands as a powerful testament to the strength and resilience of women navigating these societal constraints. Through its pages, I have sought to explore the multifaceted challenges women face and to challenge the assumptions and myths that have long defined their lives.

Drawing from real-life case studies, this book delves into the complexities of breaking stereotypes and confronting deeply ingrained perceptions that limit women's potential. Each story/Mithya serves as a mirror to broader societal issues, reflecting not only the struggles but also the triumphs of those who dare to defy conventional norms.

As you embark on this story, my invitation to you is simple: immerse yourself in the lives of these characters/cases, embrace their triumphs and failures, and allow their growth to inspire your own. It is my greatest hope that this novel will linger with you, offering moments of introspection long after the final page.

Thank you for joining me on this journey.

– Dr Smita Kamat Ghosh

Prologue

The world of MITHYA's.......

These myths, as ridiculous as they may seem, still creep into our thoughts, still mould our perceptions. They're not ancient relics – they breathe and shape the lives of women today, forming a silent barrier between who they are and who they could be.

Each myth, each expectation, carries a weight—a burden so heavy that it has become indistinguishable from truth. In a world that often diminishes a woman's voice, these myths weave a labyrinth of stereotypes, dictating how she should look, think, and live.

But what if we challenged these narratives? What if we dared to uncover the *Mithya*? This is not just a book; this is a call to reflection, to the power of questioning what has long been accepted as reality.

Hello, I am Sakhi—your *Sutradhar*, your guide, your friend. Not the idle friend of gossip and idle chatter—no. I stand beside you as we peel back the layers of these myths that have wrapped themselves around us. Together, we will unravel them, trace their origins, and most importantly, set ourselves free from their invisible chains.

Decoding The 5 Mithyas

1. **Mithya 1 Pink Stereotyping - Behind the Pink Veil:** Where did the idea of pink for girls originate? And why should we care?

2. **Mithya 2 Gendered Toys - Toy Stories of Silent Conditioning:** When did toys begin to speak gender, and what are they really telling us?

3. **Mithya 3 Feminine vs Feminism - The Silent War Within:** How do we honour who we are without betraying who we've been told to be?

4. **Mithya 4 Menstruation to Menopause - Breaking the Red Silence:** In a world of progress, why is menstruation still whispered about in shame?

5. **Mithya 5 Financial Literacy - Beyond the Myths:** A Pathway to Financial Empowerment: Why do myths keep women from financial independence?

As we journey through these *mithyas*, I will not ask you for answers. Instead, we will ask the questions that matter, the questions that will ultimately lead us to the truth.

Are You Ready to Begin?

The voice of Sakhi echoes softly but insistent, like a whisper in the wind:

"*Where does the truth end, and the myth begin? Can you trace the line between what is and what we've been told should be?*"

There's a world beneath the surface of our everyday lives—a world where colours, toys, and roles quietly dictate the shape of our existence. These aren't just superficial stories; they're scripts we've followed for generations, never once pausing to ask: *Is this really mine?* Or has it been written for me?

Together, we'll step into the heart of these questions. One myth at a time, we will walk through the veils that obscure our true selves, and in peeling back these layers, we will discover something deeper—something truer. The *mithyas* that once seemed so real will begin to fall away, and in their place, we will find our own stories waiting to be told.

Come. It is time to unravel the threads that bind us. It is time to reclaim the truths that belong to us.

As we embark on this journey of decoding, we are not just dismantling myths; we are redefining our narratives. We are forging a path toward liberation, where women can claim their identities without fear or shame. This is a journey of self-discovery and empowerment, where each revelation brings us closer to authenticity.

It's time to uncover the truth behind the MITHYAS. It's time to set ourselves free. Let us embark on this journey together, embracing the complexities of our stories and redefining what it means to be a girl or a woman in a world that often struggles to understand us.

It's time to uncover these myths. It's time to set ourselves free.

– Dr Smita Kamat Ghosh

Organisations That Shape Change

As I embarked on the journey of writing *Decoding MITHYA*, I found myself intertwined with several organisations that resonate deeply with the themes of empowerment and resilience. Each of these entities has played a vital role in shaping the narratives within this book, illuminating the complexities of the myths we encounter.

Mi Merak: This trademark encapsulates my life mantra, reflecting a profound belief that happiness is an internal journey, a truth echoed in the teachings of Gautam Buddha. It served as a compass, guiding me to explore the deeper meanings behind these myths.

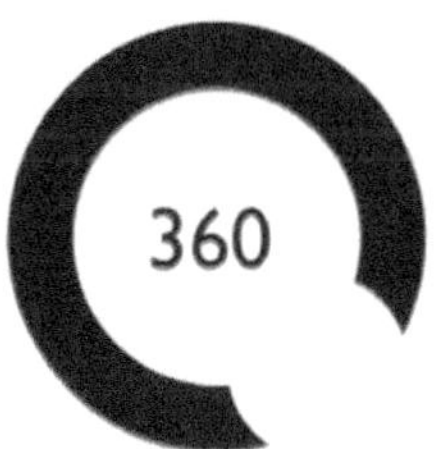

CI360: With their keen insights, this organisation helped me to identify and connect with my audience. They opened my eyes to the myriad experiences that inform our understanding, ensuring that the narratives resonate with authenticity.

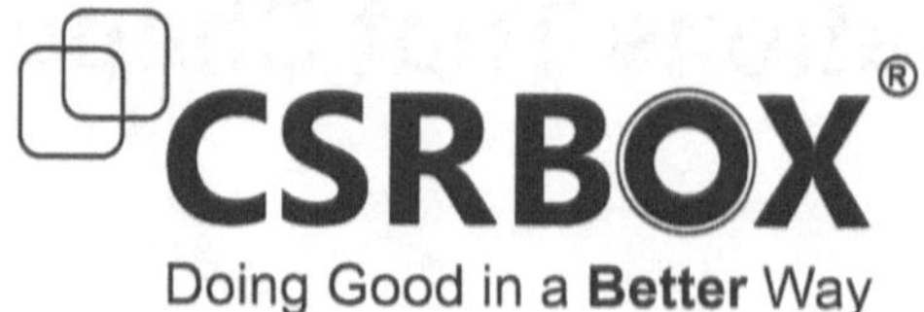

CSRBOX: In my role at CSRBOX, I was fortunate to engage in projects that brought these myths to life. It was here that I witnessed the realities faced by women, grounding my narratives in the lived experiences of those striving to challenge societal norms.

G100 Mentoring and Motivation: This initiative allowed me to connect with a network of individuals—both women and men—who are actively dismantling these myths. Their stories of courage and determination became a source of inspiration, fuelling my commitment to this cause.

Being Women: This NGO in Ahmedabad embodies the collective strength of women, driven by the motto "Together we can, together we will." They foster a community that supports women in challenging societal stereotypes and encourages resilience, echoing the themes of solidarity and empowerment central to this book.

Through these organisations, I have gained invaluable insights, each contributing to a broader understanding of the myths we face. Together, they remind us that change is not only possible but essential, urging us to confront and redefine the narratives that shape our lives.

About Author

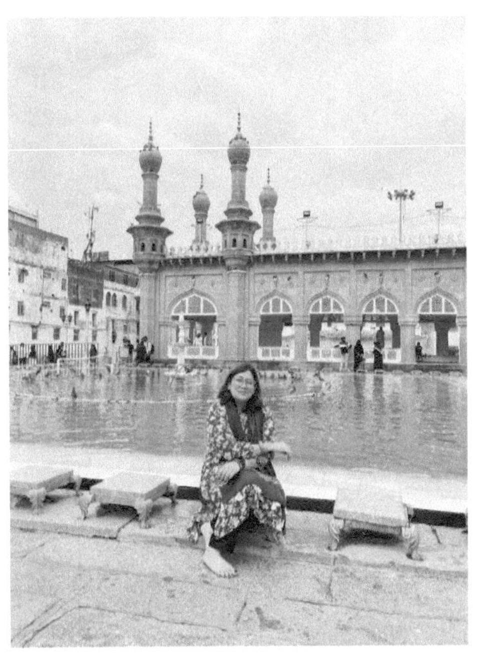

Dr Smita Kamat Ghosh (PhD, Psychology) is a dedicated psychologist, counsellor, and advocate for the upliftment of women and girls. She has worked extensively on projects centred on women's empowerment, financial literacy, and mentoring girls, challenging gender stereotypes and creating pathways for change. Her efforts also extend to supporting menstruating girls and raising awareness around this often-stigmatised issue.

In addition to her academic and advocacy work, Dr. Ghosh plays a key role in corporate social responsibility (CSR) initiatives, driving projects that promote community upliftment and foster meaningful change. She has authored numerous research papers on women's rights and empowerment. **Decoding MITHYA** is her second book, following **Mind Aid Pitara**, a psychological aid e-book. She has also contributed her expertise to a book on cybercrime, offering psychological insights for case studies.

Through her work, Dr Smita continues to inspire women to break free from societal conditioning and reclaim their rightful place in the world.

About Sakhi

 **Sakhi** is the embodiment of your alter ego, Aura—a powerful yet gentle guide through the journey of **_Decoding Mithya._** With her warm presence, she becomes a voice for women navigating the complexities of societal expectations and stereotypes. As a compassionate friend and advocate, Sakhi empowers readers to confront the myths that have long confined them.

In her narrative, Sakhi intertwines empathy with insight, inviting readers to explore their own experiences and embrace their individuality. Her journey reflects the struggles and triumphs of countless women, fostering a sense of community and resilience. Through her, readers find the strength to reshape their stories and redefine what it means to be a girl or a woman today, reminding us that true liberation begins with challenging the myths that seek to hold us back.

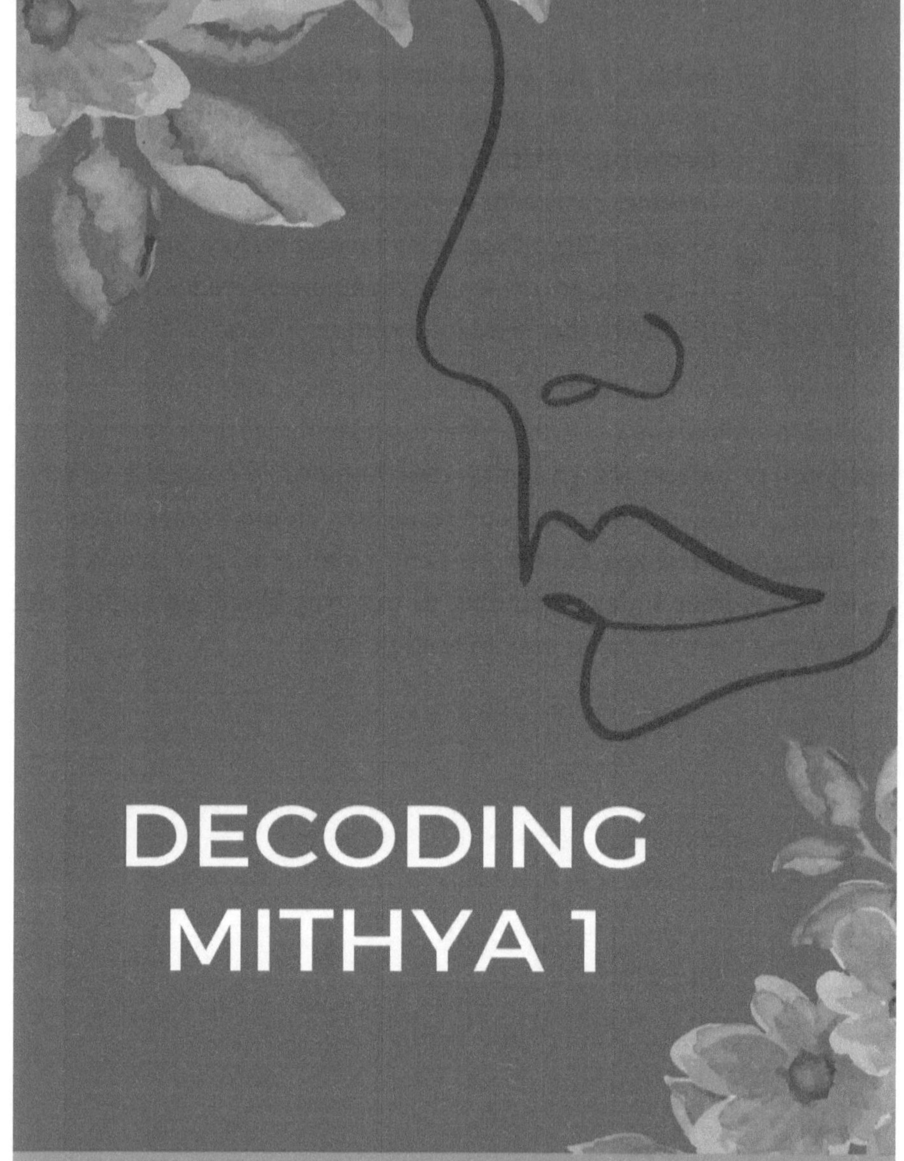

DECODING MITHYA 1
PINK STEREOTYPING

Mithya 1
Pink Stereotyping

Behind the Pink Veil

The Reality

The role of Gender in Colour Stereotypes

The Sexism in Colours

The Tsunami of Pink vs Blue, Is it Gender Bias or Media Gimmick?

Echoes of Past: The transition of Pink for Boys & Blue for Girls to Blue for boys and Pink for girls'

Need of the Day

Changing Mindset for Empowering Children by not creating Gender Colour Biases

Welcome, my dear! It's me, Sakhi, your friend, guide, and companion on this journey of unmasking myths. Today, let's talk about a MITHYA that's so deeply embedded in our world that we often don't even question it. Yes, I'm talking about the "pink for girls, blue for boys" myth.

For years, this rigid colour divide has ruled how we see the world, especially how we see our children. You see it everywhere, don't you? From baby showers to birthday parties, the pink and blue dichotomy is alive and well. But, let me tell you a secret—it wasn't always this way.

Think and Ponder

How Do You Choose Colours for Yourself?

➤ Do you tend to choose colours that are traditionally associated with your gender?

➤ How do you feel when wearing colours outside of this norm?

What Are Your Early Memories Around Colour Preferences?

➤ Do you recall a time when someone steered your colour preferences towards or away from a colour because of your gender?

➤ How did that experience shape your relationship with colours as you grew older?

How Do You Perceive Others Based on Colour Choices?

➤ When you see someone wearing colours that don't align with societal gender norms, what thoughts come to mind?

➤ How do you react internally to a boy in pink or a girl in blue?

What Are Your Colour Choices for Others?

➤ When buying gifts or clothing for children, do you instinctively choose pink for girls and blue for boys?

➤ Why do you think you make these choices?

Last Few Questions – Think

What Impact Do You Think Colour Stereotyping Has on Children?

➤ How do you think these rigid colour associations influence a child's self-expression and confidence?

Can You Reframe Colours in a Non-Gendered Way?

➢ When you think about colours like pink and blue, can you attribute new, non-gendered meanings to them? What would that look like?

Reflecting on these questions will help you understand how deeply the pink and blue divide runs, and why it's time to break free from it. Let's continue exploring the historical context and modern realities of this MITHYA.

Let's travel back to a time when colours were free, unshackled by the weight of gender. Let's turn the pages of history to a chapter that has long been forgotten.

Back to the Past: When Blue Was Feminine

There was a time, long ago, when blue was not the strong, masculine symbol it is today. Picture a world where blue was considered delicate, soft, and gentle—a colour of grace and purity. It wasn't the blue of warriors or the endless sky. It was the blue of the Virgin Mary, draped in flowing robes, symbolising serenity and motherhood. Blue carried the essence of calm, of femininity. It was not strength that blue signified, but an ethereal softness.

And then there was pink. It's hard to imagine now, but pink wasn't always seen as the colour of delicate femininity. Back then, pink was a powerful colour, bold and vivid, a diluted version of red—the colour of fire, passion, and war. Red was a symbol of power, of courage, and its lighter cousin, pink, was linked to boys. Yes, pink was for boys, carrying with it the echoes of bravery, a certain youthful boldness.

Surprising, isn't it? To think of a time when pink was meant to clothe the strong and blue was reserved for the gentle. But then, as time passed, society slowly altered its course. The marketing engines of the 20th century began to hum with new ideas, casting pink as the gentle, nurturing colour of girls and blue as the stoic, dependable hue for boys. It wasn't a natural shift—it was orchestrated, driven by commerce, a decision made in boardrooms rather than nurseries. By the 1950s, this transformation was complete. The once arbitrary, fluid association between colours had solidified into cultural law.

But the real truth? The truth was always simpler, hidden beneath layers of consumerism and societal expectation.

The Real Truth: No Colours Were Gendered

Let me take you back even further before this colour-coding ever began. Before pink and blue took on their modern meanings, babies—both boys and girls—were dressed in the same colours: neutral shades, primarily white. Imagine a time when a child's clothing was chosen not to define them, but simply to serve a purpose. White was easy to bleach, to clean, to reuse. There was no need to assign significance to it. It was practical, and that was enough.

In those days, no one thought to colour-code a newborn's destiny. A baby was a baby, their future unwritten, free from the restrictions that today's world imposes. There were no whispered fears of making boys too soft or girls too bold. Colours had no agenda, no meaning. Pastels themselves didn't come into fashion until the 19th century, and even then, there was no hard-and-fast rule about who should wear what. Boys could wear pink, girls could wear blue, and the earth kept spinning just the same.

But somewhere along the way, society, ever eager to categorise and define, decided that colours could shape identities. Slowly, over years and decades, the myth began to build. Pink became soft, nurturing, delicate—the colour of girls. And blue became strong, steady, serious— the colour of boys. It didn't happen all at once, but like a trickle of water that gradually wears away stone, these ideas took root. What was once an innocent choice of fabric turned into a declaration of who a child was meant to become.

And so, we find ourselves here today, living with this MITHYA, this falsehood that we've woven so tightly into our culture. Yet if we look closely, we can still see the truth. No colour was ever born with gender. Blue was never masculine; pink was never feminine. These were just colours—innocent, free, and unburdened by the roles we've imposed upon them.

Marketing Myths: When Retailers Took Over

Then came the age of marketing. Advertisers saw a chance to capitalise on parental love and desire to prepare for their babies' arrival. Suddenly, retailers had a whole new opportunity—to tailor products based on gender. And so, pink and blue found their way back into the limelight, pushed not by tradition, but by a desire to sell more cribs, clothes, toys, and accessories. In the blink of an eye, we were back to square one— pink for girls, blue for boys.

Do you see what happened here? What was once a choice based on fashion trends became a full-fledged gender stereotype, drilled into our minds from the moment we are born. This is the MITHYA we've inherited—a myth created for profit, not for truth.

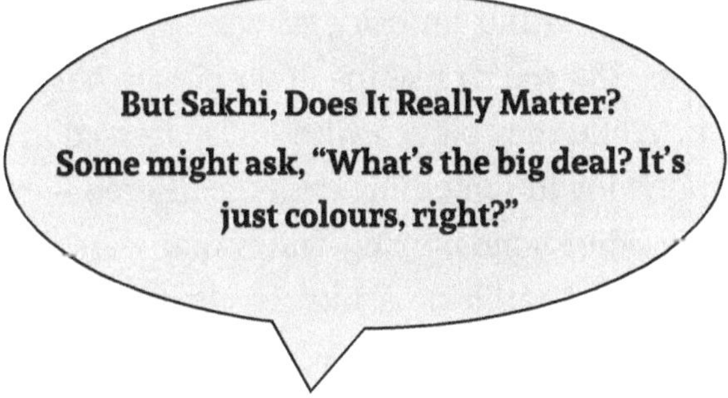

I hear you, but trust me, it matters. Think about it—these colours are not just about aesthetics. They are the foundation of gender stereotypes. We teach children, from the earliest days, that pink is for girls, that girls are supposed to be gentle, emotional, and nurturing. Meanwhile, boys are supposed to be assertive, tough, and independent—just like the colour blue. It's not just a choice of colour—it's an invisible force shaping identities.

As your Sutradhar-Sakhi, I urge you to remember this. The lines society draws are not carved in stone. They are made by us, and they can be erased by us. So, ask yourself:

> **What if we let colors be what they were always meant to be—just colors, nothing more?**
>
> **What if we allowed ourselves to see the world through a prism free of these artificial boundaries?"**

As we travel deeper into this exploration of colours and identities, let me share a story. Not just any story, but one that shows how deeply this myth can wound.

The Story of Dreams Stifled by Colour

Priya was a girl full of life and curiosity, growing up in a small, sun-soaked town in Rajasthan. She wasn't like the other girls in her neighbourhood, and she knew it. While they played with dolls, dressed in soft pinks and pastels, Priya found joy in something entirely different—mechanics. She loved working with her hands, fixing things that were broken. Whether it was her father's old radio or a bicycle chain that refused to turn, Priya's nimble fingers knew exactly what to do. The excitement that sparked in her eyes when she opened up gadgets, when she could see the inner workings, was a kind of joy few understood.

But as Priya grew older, she began to feel the weight of the world pressing down on her. What had once been admiration for her skills slowly morphed into murmurs of concern. "Shouldn't you be playing with dolls, Priya?" her neighbours asked. "Why aren't you interested in things girls usually like?" Her family, too, began to worry. "You're always around tools, always dressed like a boy," they said. "It's time to grow up."

> **"Shouldn't you be playing with dolls, Priya?"**
>
> **"Why aren't you interested in things girls usually like?"**
>
> **"You're always around tools, always dressed like a boy,"**
> **they said**

And slowly, the world began to shape her. The mechanics kit she once cherished was replaced with frilly dresses and dolls she had no interest in. The pink clothes she had never asked for became her new uniform, and with it, Priya started losing pieces of herself. The questions, the stares, the societal expectations—each one chipped away at her passion. She began hiding her interests, tucking away the part of her that loved to tinker, to create. She traded her overalls for skirts, her tools for pink accessories, trying so hard to fit into a mould that never belonged to her.

But it wasn't just about pink. It was about a world that had already decided who Priya should be—before she even had the chance to discover it for herself. Her dream of becoming an engineer, something she had once carried with such pride, began to fade. Not because she lacked the talent, but because this MITHYA—this societal lie about what girls should be—had stolen her courage.

Priya's story is just one of many. There are countless girls like her, whose dreams are stifled not by their abilities, but by these artificial constraints that tell them what's "appropriate." But this isn't just a story about girls. Boys, too, bear the brunt of this myth.

I remember another story, one of a boy named Arjun. Arjun, unlike his classmates, loved wearing pink. His favourite shirt was a soft blush colour, and it made him feel confident and joyful. But the moment he stepped into school wearing it, the teasing began. "You look like a girl!" "Pink is for sissies!" "Are you gay?"—the words were sharp, cutting into his sense of self. Arjun, like so many boys, was told that by choosing pink, he was choosing something less masculine, less worthy.

He wore the shirt only once.

This MITHYA doesn't just imprison girls; it traps boys, too, forcing them into rigid roles. Boys who show softness, boys who prefer pink, are often labelled as weak, effeminate, or worse. And girls who dare to wear blue or love sports are branded as tomboys, as if their choices make them less of a girl, as if colour could somehow define who they are at their core.

Do you see now, my dear? How dangerous these labels are? It might seem harmless, just colours, but it's so much more. It shapes our identities, limits our dreams, and boxes us into narrow definitions of what is 'acceptable.' By labelling pink as "for girls" and blue as "for boys," we're not just choosing colours. We're choosing who they're allowed to be, long before they have the chance to figure it out for themselves.

What happens when a little boy loves pink? He's told it's "girly," that he shouldn't like it. When a girl prefers blue, she's labelled a "tomboy," as if being herself is something to be corrected. These small things grow into larger issues of gender inequality. We start enforcing roles before children even have the chance to discover who they truly are.

So, I ask you, can we truly afford to keep living by these myths? Can we not allow children to grow, free from the weight of colour-coded boxes, free to explore all the possibilities the world has to offer?"

Breaking Free: Why It's Time to Let Go

As your Sakhi, I ask you—why should we let colours define who we are or who our children become? Colours are nothing but reflections of light. They're meant to bring joy, vibrancy, and beauty to our lives. They shouldn't be chains that bind us into roles we never chose.

The truth is, gendered colours are a relic of a time we've moved past—or at least, we should have. In the 1960s, during the women's liberation movement, there was a push to throw these stereotypes out the window. For a while, it seemed like we had broken free. But as gender-specific marketing gained traction again, we found ourselves back where we started.

The World Beyond Pink and Blue: ROYGBIV

Let's think of the rainbow—ROYGBIV. Seven colours, each one unique and beautiful. Why, then, do we limit ourselves to just pink and blue? There's an entire spectrum out there, and it's time we embrace it. Just as every colour has a place in the rainbow, so too should every child be free to choose their own path.

Together, let's step beyond the pink and blue divide. Let's create a world where colours don't define us—where we define who we are, with love, pride, and freedom. As your Sakhi, I'll be here with you, every step of the way.

So, what do you say? Let's shatter this MITHYA, once and for all. Just like Priya, we all deserve to live free of these constraints, to chase our true passions, and to celebrate who we really are.

Breaking the Stereotype: Shifting Mindsets and Perceptions

I am Sakhi, your Sutradhar, and together, we'll explore how to dismantle the colour-coded myths that shape our lives. This journey begins not with grand gestures but with small, deliberate actions that slowly erode the stereotypes we've unknowingly upheld. Just as a single drop of water can carve its way through stone over time, small efforts can break down the deep-seated belief that pink is for girls and blue is for boys. Let's walk through these steps to challenge the norms, shift mindsets, and embrace a more inclusive way of thinking.

➤ **Unmasking the Colours: A Week of Colour Rebellion**

Your Step: For the next 7 days, dive into the unfamiliar. Women, drape yourselves in shades of blue, green, or grey. Men, reach for pink, lavender, or even floral patterns. Step into these colours with intention—observe how you feel as you go about your day. Did you feel out of place, or did the colours speak to your boldness? Jot down your reflections. Were there comments from others? Did they make you question your choice?

Why This Matters: This activity is more than a wardrobe change; it's a challenge to long-standing norms. By stepping into colours that society has labelled "off-limits," you directly confront the MITHYA that has subtly shaped your choices. As you peel back these layers, you begin to see how easily we've been trained to follow invisible rules. This simple act of rebellion opens your mind, allowing you to question the labels that once dictated how you dressed and, more importantly, how you viewed yourself.

➤ **The Gift of Freedom: Moving Beyond Gendered Choices**

Your Step: The next time you're shopping for a gift—whether for a birthday or just because—pause. Instead of heading straight to the pink or blue aisles, look for gifts that speak to curiosity, creativity, or fun. Consider a toolset for a girl, or a cooking kit for a boy. Reflect on the experience afterward. Did the shelves pull you towards gendered sections? Did you feel a sense of discomfort picking a "non-traditional" toy?

Why This Matters: Gift-giving is more than an exchange of objects— it's an opportunity to shape a child's view of the world. By consciously rejecting the typical gender-coded gifts, you're sending a message that curiosity and passion are not defined by colours. This shift, though small, chips away at the MITHYA children absorb early on, planting seeds of freedom where rigid norms once stood. It's a gesture of love that extends beyond the present itself, giving a child permission to explore who they truly are.

➢ **Imagining a World Without Colour Boundaries: A Visionary Escape**

Your Step: Find a peaceful spot, close your eyes, and imagine a world where colours aren't bound to gender. Picture boys playing in pink shirts, girls racing toy cars in a mix of blues and reds. Imagine yourself walking down the street in a colour you wouldn't normally choose. What does this world feel like? What do the children in your life look like in this liberated space? Let your imagination flow freely, unencumbered by the expectations you've been conditioned to accept.

Why This Matters: Visualisation breaks the chains of conformity. By actively imagining a world where colours hold no boundaries, you begin to internalise this freedom. This exercise trains your mind to look past societal constraints, showing you how artificial these boundaries really are. The more you embrace this vision, the easier it becomes to let go of old mindsets, eventually bringing that imagined freedom into your daily life.

➢ **Rewriting Colour Stories: A Mental Shift**

Your Step: Throughout your day, actively challenge how you view colours. When you see a soft pink, think of its boldness, of its strength. When you see blue, reframe it as a calming force, serene but powerful. Each time you catch yourself labelling a colour as "feminine" or "masculine," pause. Reflect on what societal conditioning has done to your perception. Then, consciously rewrite that narrative in your mind.

Why This Matters: This exercise is like mental strength training. It forces you to rewire how your brain has been taught to associate certain colours with specific traits. Slowly, you begin to break down the automatic judgements you've learned over time, helping to free yourself from the colour-coded limitations that influence both you and those around you. Over time, this shift in perspective transforms your interactions with the world, allowing you to see beyond the superficial barriers of colour.

➢ **Conversations of Curiosity: Guiding Children to Freedom**

Your Step: Engage the children in your life with open-ended questions about their favourite colours and toys, without tying them to gender. Ask, "Why do you like that colour?" or "What's exciting about this toy?" Celebrate their choices, whatever they may be, and encourage them to follow their preferences. Notice how easily they express themselves without the weight of societal expectations if given the chance.

Why This Matters: Children are natural explorers, and by offering them a judgement-free space to express their likes and dislikes, you open the door to authentic self-discovery. This conversation not only helps them break the mould but also shapes the way they will approach identity in the future. By removing the gendered lens through which they view colour and toys, you give them the gift of seeing the world as it truly is—a place where they are free to be whoever they wish, without limits.

The Ripple Effect: Rewriting the Colour Narrative

Each activity moves us closer to a world where colour doesn't define or confine us. By taking these steps, you contribute to dismantling the deeply ingrained MITHYA, not just for yourself but for the generations that follow. This shift doesn't happen overnight, but with each mindful choice, we carve a path toward freedom—one where colour serves only as a tool for expression, not a box that limits our potential.

In reclaiming our relationship with colour, we reclaim a part of ourselves long hidden beneath the layers of societal expectation. Together, we strip away the myth that has silenced our individuality and, in doing so, open the doors to a brighter, more vibrant world.

A Final Reflection: Embracing Authenticity Beyond Colour

As we explore the myths surrounding colour, we are guided by the wisdom of the Bhagavad Gita:

"न हंति न हन्यमि, न हन्ति हन्ति यं:|"

"The soul kills not, nor is it killed; it is eternal, indestructible, and ever-changing."

– Bhagavad Gita 2.19

This verse encourages us to understand that our essence transcends physical attributes and societal labels. Our true selves are not confined by the colours we wear or the roles society imposes upon us. Instead, we should look beyond these superficial norms to discover our authentic identity.

The evolution of colour associations vividly illustrates how arbitrary and mutable these norms can be. Historically, blue was once associated with girls, partly due to its religious symbolism and connections to purity. Pink, meanwhile, was considered strong and masculine. It wasn't until the mid-20th century that advertising and marketing campaigns redefined these colours into the gendered norms we recognise today. This shift was not a natural progression but a manufactured one, designed to fit commercial needs.

Cultural Influences and Historical Figures

In the 18th century, French fashion, driven by Louis XV, played a significant role in shaping colour norms. The King's adoption of pastel colours, including blue and pink, initially had no gendered connotations. Pink was still often associated with boys, viewed as a lighter version of red. It wasn't until post-World War II marketing strategies, notably by companies like Mattel, that pink was aggressively marketed for girls and blue for boys. This commercialisation entrenched colour norms that continue to shape societal expectations.

Challenging the Norms

Annie Besant, a prominent figure in Indian social reform, championed women's education and rights, challenging gender norms of her time. Her advocacy for gender equality went beyond traditional roles, promoting a vision where women could pursue education and empowerment irrespective of societal expectations.

Mahatma Gandhi's choice of traditional khadi clothing and his rejection of Western fashion norms emphasised practicality and personal values over colour and fashion. His approach highlighted that personal identity and beliefs transcend societal stereotypes.

Modern Day Figures

In contemporary India, individuals like Priya and Aarav exemplify the spirit of challenging outdated norms. Priya, passionate about engineering despite societal expectations, and Aarav, who proudly wore traditionally "feminine" colours, embody the courage to defy restrictive norms. Their stories remind us that true freedom lies in expressing oneself authentically, beyond imposed limitations.

These examples reveal that colour norms have been shaped by a mix of cultural, historical, and commercial influences. As we move forward, we should remember that colours, while beautiful and varied, should not constrain our identities or aspirations. Embracing the full spectrum of human experience means rejecting colour stereotypes and celebrating our unique selves.

Breaking the myth of pink for girls and blue for boys isn't about rejecting the beauty of colours but reclaiming our right to choose and express ourselves freely. As we embrace every hue and facet of our being, we honour the rich diversity of human expression.

Let us step into this vibrant world with open hearts and minds, celebrating the boundless possibilities that come from being true to ourselves. Colours do not define us; we define ourselves. In doing so, we embrace the full richness of our existence, unshackled by outdated stereotypes.

Colours do not define us. We define who we are. Let's shatter the myth of pink for girls and blue for boys and embrace the full spectrum of who we can be.

Activity: Redefining Colour Boundaries

As we reach the end of our chapter on colour stereotypes, let us embark on a journey to explore and question our own perceptions. This activity invites you to look beyond traditional colour norms and embrace a more nuanced understanding of identity.

Objective: To delve into your personal associations with colour and gender, and to imagine a world where these boundaries are more fluid.

Materials Needed

➤ Large sheet of paper or poster board.

➤ Markers, crayons, or coloured pencils.

➤ Sticky notes.

➤ Tape or glue.

Activity Steps

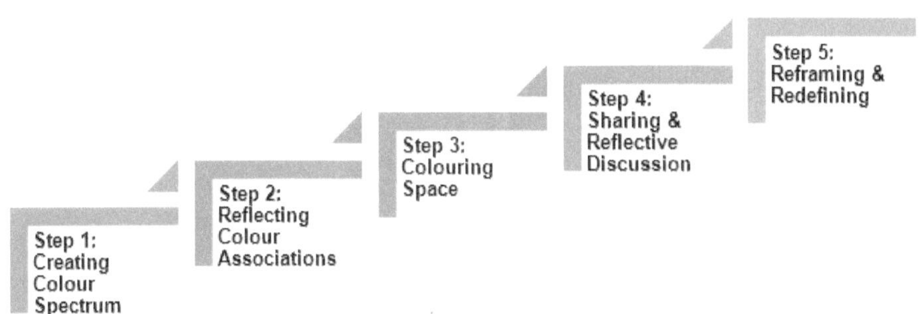

Step 1: Create Your Colour Spectrum

On a large sheet of paper, draw a vibrant spectrum of colours, extending from the soft pastels to the bold and bright hues. Let the colours blend into one another, creating a rich tapestry that represents the full range of human experience. This spectrum symbolises the diversity of our identities, unconfined by traditional norms.

Step 2: Reflect on Your Colour Associations

Pause for a moment and think about the colours you associate with specific genders. Consider how these associations have shaped your perceptions and choices. Write down your thoughts on sticky notes. For instance, you might label pink with words like "delicate" or "feminine," while blue might be tagged with "strong" or "masculine."

Example: If pink brings to mind images of softness and gentleness, note this down. Reflect on how this colour, often reserved for girls, contrasts with your personal experience.

Step 3: Colour Your Space

Select a colour from your spectrum that resonates with you. This might be a colour that reflects a facet of your personality or a quality you value. Use markers or crayons to fill a section of your paper with this colour, allowing yourself to immerse in its hue and what it represents for you.

Example: If you feel a connection to green for its associations with growth and renewal, let this colour dominate a part of your paper. As you colour, think about how this choice defies or aligns with traditional expectations.

Step 4: Share and Discuss

If you're participating in this activity with others, take the opportunity to share your chosen colours and the reasons behind your selections. Discuss how these choices either uphold or challenge traditional stereotypes. This exchange can provide valuable insights into how deeply ingrained societal norms shape our perceptions and how we can collectively reshape them.

Reflective Discussion Prompts

> What motivated your colour choice? Reflect on why you chose a particular colour and how it resonates with your personal identity or values.

> How do you feel about traditional colour associations? Share whether your choice reinforces or defies common stereotypes about gender and colour.

> What new perspectives have emerged from this discussion? Explore how your peers' choices and rationales have shifted your understanding of colour norms and their implications.

For Example:

Reader A: Might choose blue for its associations with calmness and clarity, challenging the notion that blue is exclusively for boys. Discuss how this choice reflects broader qualities and how it feels to defy traditional norms.

Reader B: Could select pink to symbolise creativity and energy, opposing the stereotype that pink is only for girls. Explore how this choice broadens the meaning of pink and what it signifies about personal expression.

Alternative Approach

If you are engaging in this activity solo, consider journaling your thoughts and reflections about your colour choices. Reflect on how your selected colours align with or diverge from traditional gender stereotypes. Then, reach out to friends or family to share your reflections and invite them to share theirs. This dialogue, even if not face-to-face, can enrich your understanding and foster a broader discussion on colour and identity.

Example of Solo Reflection

➢ Write about why you chose a specific colour and how it represents your values or traits.

➢ Note any shifts in your perspective regarding traditional colour norms.

➢ Reach out to others through social media or personal conversations to discuss these reflections and gain additional insights.

Step 5: Reframe and Redefine

In the remaining space on your paper, imagine a world where colours are not bound by gendered expectations. Picture a world where individuals freely choose colours and express themselves without fear of judgement.

How would this new world look?

How might it feel?

Example Vision: Imagine a school where children choose their uniforms in a rainbow of colours, and a playground where toys are as diverse as the colours themselves. Reflect on how such a world would liberate everyone from the constraints of colour-based stereotypes.

How This Activity Helps

Encourages Self-Reflection: This exercise allows you to explore and confront your own biases, deepening your understanding of how colour norms have shaped your identity.

Fosters Open Dialogue: Sharing your experiences and choices helps to unravel stereotypes and promotes a more inclusive perspective on gender and colour.

Promotes Reimagining Norms: By envisioning a world free from colour-based constraints, you foster creative thinking and contribute to breaking down outdated stereotypes.

This activity is a chance for everyone to step beyond traditional labels and embrace the full spectrum of human experience. It's about celebrating who we are, unshackled by the constraints of outdated norms.

Let us, with open hearts and minds, venture into this colourful exploration, celebrating the richness of our identities beyond the bounds of pink and blue.

With warm reflection,

Sakhi

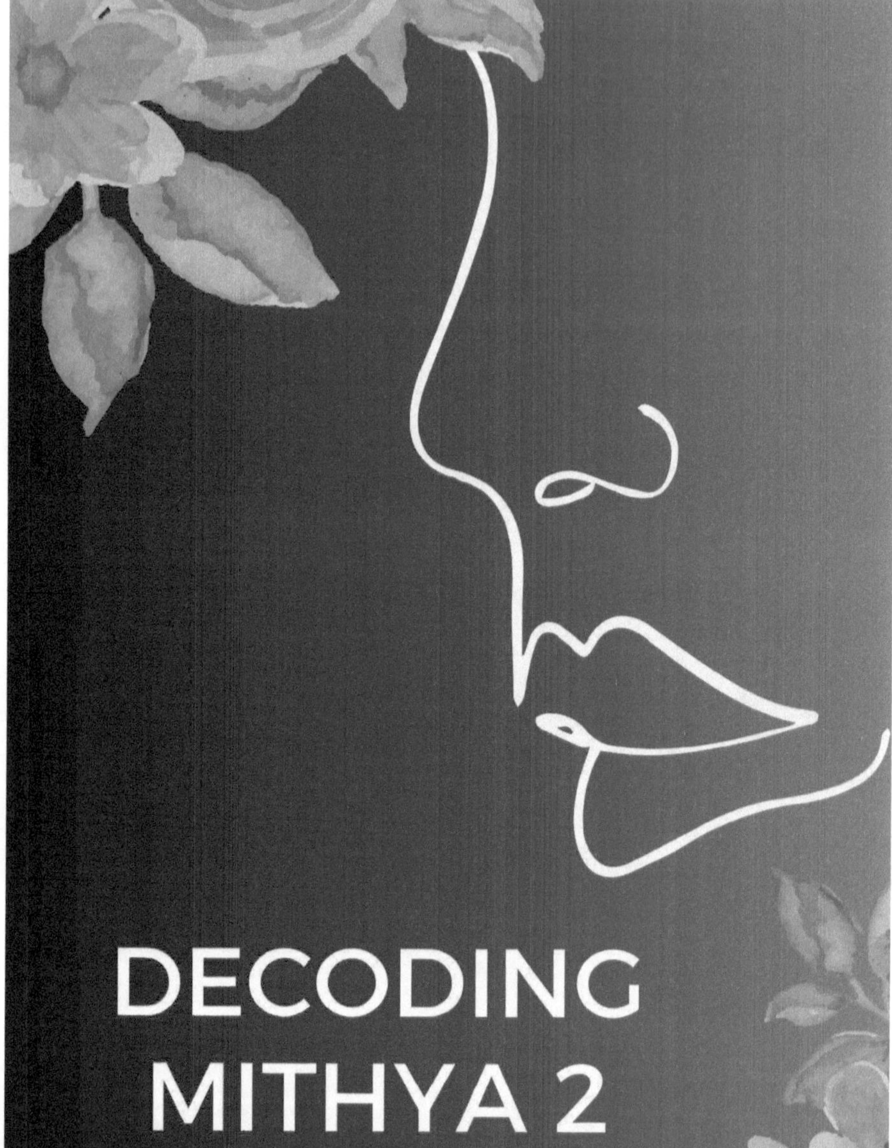

DECODING
MITHYA 2
GENDERED TOYS

Mithya 2
Gendered Toys

Toy Stories of Silent Conditioning

> Understanding why how and when Toys became Gendered
>
> Toy Stories over the century
>
> Gender stereotype toys effects on children's development
>
> Changing the Gender label (Stereotype) on Toys & Breaking the Gender Binary
>
> "The toys we give children today shape the stories they tell themselves tomorrow." — Unknown

Having examined and deconstructed **Mithya 1: Pink Stereotypes,** we now turn our attention to another significant facet of gendered expectations. It's me, **Sakhi,** your **Sutradhar,** guiding you through another chapter of our journey, where we unveil the hidden dynamics of play. Today, we'll explore the colourful and complex world of toys—a domain where imagination meets societal expectations. Beneath the surface of these cherished playthings, **gender constraints** quietly persist.

Before we dive deeper, let's take a moment to reflect on a few questions that may reshape our understanding:

Reflective Questions

Toy Memories

➢ Think back to the toys you played with as a child. Were you encouraged to play with certain toys based on your gender?

➢ How did those toys shape your interests or sense of self? Do you feel your choices were limited or expanded by the types of toys available to you?

Unconscious Bias in Gifting

➢ When buying toys for children, do you automatically gravitate towards dolls or kitchen sets for girls and cars or building blocks for boys? Why do you make these choices?

➢ Do you feel any hesitation or discomfort when a child plays with a toy that doesn't align with their gender? What thoughts arise when this happens?

Gender Roles and Career Aspirations

➢ Think about how traditional gendered toys might have influenced career aspirations for boys and girls. Have you seen children around you gravitate towards careers based on the toys they are encouraged to play with?

➢ How might offering gender-neutral or non-gendered toys impact a child's future career choices and skills development?

Societal Expectations

➢ Do you find yourself or others reinforcing gender roles through toys? For instance, do you encourage girls to play "house" while encouraging boys to play "hero" roles?

➢ Are there subtle ways in which you or others in your environment restrict children's choices based on toy preferences?

Breaking Patterns

➢ Reflect on a moment when you allowed a child (or yourself) to play with a toy typically associated with another gender.

➢ How did it make you feel? What was the child's reaction? How did others react, if present?

Now that we've explored these questions, let's journey into the world of **Gendered Toys,** uncover their influence, and discover how we can break free from these restrictive moulds.

The Origins of Gendered Toys

The Hidden Narratives of Play

Play is often considered the purest form of freedom and joy, a sacred space where the burdens of the adult world fade away. Yet, if we peer closer, beyond the surface of carefree laughter and imaginative games, we begin to unravel the complexities woven into this seemingly innocent realm. Toys—those vibrant, cheerful objects of fun—are laden with societal messages and expectations. They transcend mere playthings, emerging as vessels that carry deep-seated cultural narratives about gender roles.

In a time not so distant, the phenomenon of gendered toys was almost non-existent. Children played with whatever captured their imaginations—a wooden horse might gallop into the hands of a girl just as readily as a boy, and a simple set of blocks welcomed any child eager to build. The freedom of play knew no boundaries, transcending gender. But as the 20th century dawned, a significant shift began to take shape, revealing a landscape where toys were meticulously categorised.

With the rise of marketing and advertising, toys started to be presented through a gendered lens. This shift was not an organic reflection of evolving societal values but rather a calculated strategy by advertisers and toy manufacturers, designed to capture distinct consumer bases and maximise profits. The bright, gender-coded packaging—pink for girls and blue for boys—became a hallmark of this new era, forever altering the way children interacted with their toys.

Dolls, often associated with nurturing and domesticity, were promoted as the ideal choice for girls, subtly instilling the notion that their roles were to be gentle and caring. Meanwhile, action figures, building sets, and cars were marketed towards boys, aligning with an adventurous spirit that suggested strength and exploration. In this carefully constructed narrative, children absorbed the expectations that came packaged with their toys, shaping their identities in ways that echoed the biases of the adult world.

As we reflect on this evolution, we uncover the profound implications of such conditioning. Play, which should be a sanctuary of creativity and self-expression, becomes a stage for societal norms to play out, reinforcing outdated stereotypes that dictate what is deemed appropriate for each gender. This manufactured dichotomy not only stifles the individuality of children but also limits their potential to explore the vast landscapes of their imaginations without the constraints of gender.

In recognising these hidden narratives, we must advocate for a world where play remains truly untainted—a world where every child can embrace their interests without the weight of societal expectations. By challenging these constructs, we pave the way for a more inclusive understanding of play, allowing children to redefine their identities beyond the limitations imposed by gendered toys. As we move forward, let us encourage a celebration of diversity in play, fostering environments where every child can thrive, free from the shadows of preconceived notions.

The Impact of Gendered Toys on Development

The impact of gendered toys extends far beyond childhood play. These toys are not just about entertainment; they play a critical role in shaping children's perceptions of themselves and their place in the world. When children are consistently exposed to gendered toys, they internalise the associated roles and expectations. This has profound implications for their interests, aspirations, and self-concept.

Consider a young girl who is given dolls and kitchen sets while her male peers receive toolkits and action figures. Over time, she might come to view domestic roles as her primary domain, believing that her value lies in nurturing and caretaking. Similarly, a boy who is encouraged to play with trucks and superheroes may develop an identity centred around strength and action, potentially overlooking other aspects of his personality and interests.

This early socialisation can limit the scope of children's aspirations. Girls who are primarily exposed to toys that emphasise beauty, caregiving, and domesticity might feel subtly guided away from careers in science or engineering. Boys, who are encouraged to play with toys that emphasise aggression and competition, might shy away from professions in nurturing fields or arts.

The influence of gendered toys extends far beyond mere preference. These toys shape how children see themselves and their potential, often reinforcing societal expectations rather than encouraging genuine interests. To illustrate this impact, let me share with you a poignant story from the bustling city of Pune.

In the vibrant heart of Pune, amidst the colours of local festivals and the hum of busy streets, there was a quaint toy shop named "Imaginative Treasures." The shop was known for its enchanting array of toys and its owner, Mr. Rajesh, who was deeply passionate about fostering creativity in children. Yet, despite his dedication, Mr. Rajesh observed a troubling trend: the shop's shelves were increasingly divided along gender lines. Pink dolls were neatly arranged for girls, while blue action figures dominated the boys' section.

This division caught the attention of 2 special children—Anaya and Rohan. Anaya, with her bright eyes and boundless imagination, loved to dream of adventures and build fantastical creations. She saw herself as an engineer, constructing intricate models and exploring the far reaches of her imagination. However, the toys available to her seemed to limit her dreams, confined to traditional female roles and devoid of the construction sets she yearned for.

Rohan, a sensitive and nurturing boy, found joy in caring for his pets and expressing his compassion. Yet, the toys marketed to boys appeared at odds with his gentle nature. He longed for toys that reflected his love for caregiving, but those were tucked away in the girls' section, leaving him to grapple with a sense of incongruence between his interests and societal expectations.

Recognising the impact of these gendered divisions, Mr Rajesh decided to challenge the norm. With determination, he redesigned his shop. The new layout featured toys organised not by gender, but by interests and passions. Building sets, space exploration kits, and nurturing toys were all displayed together, inviting children to explore their true interests without the constraints of gender labels.

Anaya, now free to choose toys that matched her love for engineering and exploration, felt a surge of renewed confidence. She eagerly selected construction kits and scientific tools, her heart brimming with excitement and possibility. For her, the store had become a place where her dreams were not only acknowledged but celebrated.

Rohan also found solace in the transformed shop. He chose toys that aligned with his caring nature, feeling supported rather than restricted by traditional gender norms. The new arrangement allowed him to embrace his nurturing side openly, without the pressure to conform to expectations that didn't fit his true self.

Together with Mr Rajesh, Anaya and Rohan embarked on a journey to advocate for a world where toys reflected individual passions rather than gendered stereotypes. Their story became a beacon of change, inspiring others to see beyond colour-coded limitations and embrace a world where creativity and potential are limitless.

This tale from Pune is a powerful reminder of how gendered toys can shape—and sometimes stifle—our dreams. Yet, it also shows that change is possible when we challenge these constraints and create spaces that nurture the full spectrum of children's interests and aspirations.

Challenges and Opportunities in Promoting Gender-Neutral Toys

The quest for gender-neutral toys, while filled with promise, is fraught with significant challenges. At the heart of this journey lies a battleground of deeply entrenched stereotypes and resistance from traditional manufacturers. Yet, amidst these obstacles, the landscape also teems with opportunities and innovations that guide us toward a more inclusive future.

Challenges

The journey toward gender-neutral toys begins with confronting the deep-seated stereotypes that permeate our society. Toys have long served as instruments for reinforcing gender roles, with cultural expectations dictating not only what children play with but how they perceive their own interests and abilities. A toy truck, for instance, may symbolise adventure and strength, while a doll is often seen as a representation of nurturing and domesticity. These associations are so deeply ingrained that challenging them requires significant shifts in societal attitudes and marketing strategies.

Moreover, traditional manufacturers pose a substantial barrier. Many have built their brands around gender-specific toys, creating a business model that thrives on the segmentation of products aimed at distinct demographics. The lucrative market for pink toys for girls and blue toys for boys serves as a powerful incentive to uphold these outdated norms. Shifting these entrenched practices involves not only persuading manufacturers of the potential financial benefits of gender-neutral toys but also overcoming the inertia of established production processes and marketing strategies.

Opportunities

Despite these hurdles, the road to gender-neutral toys is not without its bright spots. Advocacy campaigns and grassroots movements are leading the charge for change, shining a light on the importance of breaking down gender barriers. Organisations and individuals committed to this cause are raising awareness and promoting inclusive practices. Their efforts range from public awareness campaigns to educational programmes that encourage children to explore a diverse array of interests, free from the constraints of gender labels.

Innovative companies are emerging as beacons of hope in this landscape. These trailblazers are redefining the toy industry by creating products that celebrate diversity and promote gender equality. For instance, brands like GoldieBlox are designing toys that invite girls to delve into engineering and science, while others are producing dolls that represent a wide spectrum of races, abilities, and family structures. These products not only broaden the play options available to children but also challenge traditional gender norms through thoughtful design and marketing.

There is also a growing recognition of the importance of representation in toys. As more parents and educators advocate for gender-neutral options, toy manufacturers are beginning to respond. This shift is not solely about removing gender labels; it involves embracing a new way of thinking about play. It calls for the creation of toys that foster creativity, problem-solving, and empathy, regardless of the child's gender.

The journey toward a more inclusive world of play is undeniably long, marked by both obstacles and opportunities. However, each step forward—whether a new gender-neutral toy line or a successful advocacy campaign—brings us closer to a reality where toys are celebrated for their ability to inspire and educate rather than constrain.

In this evolving landscape, the blend of persistent advocacy, innovative design, and changing consumer attitudes creates a hopeful horizon. As we support and celebrate these efforts, we contribute to a future where play knows no bounds, and every child can revel in joy and discovery, exploring a world of limitless possibilities.

So, dear readers, let us engage in this transformative journey together, embracing the potential that lies within each child and ensuring that their play reflects their true selves, unbound by the constraints of outdated expectations. Each small change we advocate for holds the power to illuminate paths of creativity, empathy, and understanding, forging a brighter tomorrow for all.

Breaking the Stereotype: Shifting Mindsets and Perceptions

> **Toy Freedom Experiment**

How to Do It: Create a "toy freedom zone" for one week. In this space, children can select any toy they wish without any influence from adults. This means no guidance, suggestions, or expectations about what they "should" play with based on gender norms. The idea is to observe their choices in a setting where societal expectations are absent.

Example: Imagine a young child, Rani, who has always been drawn to dolls because her family believes that's what girls should like. During the toy freedom experiment, Rani discovers a set of building blocks that fascinate her. She spends hours constructing elaborate structures, revealing an interest she hadn't explored before. Conversely, her brother, Sameer, who typically gravitates towards trucks, finds himself intrigued by a set of art supplies and begins to experiment with drawing.

Why It Matters: This activity helps reveal children's natural preferences and interests without the constraints of gendered expectations. It can uncover hidden talents and passions, allowing for a broader range of experiences and opportunities for children. By stepping away from stereotypes, we create a more inclusive environment that values each child's individual interests and potential.

> **Toy Shelf Reorganisation**

How to Do It: When shopping for toys, intentionally explore sections that are traditionally considered "opposite" or less stereotypical. For example, if shopping for a girl, look at toys typically marketed to boys, and vice versa. Focus on selecting items based on the child's genuine interests rather than their gender.

Example: During a shopping trip, Priya, who usually buys pink dolls for her daughter, decides to browse the "boys'" section. She picks out a science kit and a set of engineering toys, believing her daughter might enjoy them. At home, her daughter is thrilled by the new science kit, sparking an unexpected interest in experiments and problem-solving.

Why It Matters: This approach challenges traditional gender norms and encourages children to explore a wider array of interests. It fosters a more open-minded approach to play and learning, breaking down barriers that limit children's potential based on gendered expectations.

➤ Encourage Role-Swapping

How to Do It: While playing with children, suggest they try out roles or activities they wouldn't typically engage in. Encourage boys to play with dolls and girls to build with trucks or racing tracks. This could be structured as a playful challenge or a creative game.

Example: During a playdate, Anil and Meera are encouraged to swap roles: Anil takes on the role of a caregiver with a doll, while Meera builds a race track for cars. Anil discovers a new appreciation for nurturing and storytelling, while Meera enjoys the challenge of construction and problem-solving.

Why It Matters: Role-swapping introduces children to a range of experiences, promoting empathy and understanding. It helps break down rigid gender roles and encourages children to see beyond traditional expectations, fostering a more flexible and inclusive view of their abilities and interests.

➤ Neutral Toy Labelling

How to Do It: Visualise and create a toy environment where items are categorised by activity or skill rather than by gender. For example, group toys by themes like "building," "exploring," or "nurturing" rather than "for boys" or "for girls."

Example: Imagine a toy store where all toys are organised by category rather than by gender. A section for "exploration" includes science kits, telescopes, and nature kits, while "building" features blocks, construction sets, and DIY kits. This reorganisation allows children to choose toys based on their interests rather than societal labels.

Why It Matters: Neutral toy labelling helps remove the gendered constraints that limit children's play choices. It encourages them to explore a wider range of activities and interests, fostering a more inclusive environment that values creativity and exploration over traditional gender norms.

➤ Toy Reflection with Children

How to Do It: Engage in conversations with children about their toy preferences without linking them to gender. Ask them what they like about their toys and what they enjoy doing with them. Focus on aspects like creativity, fun, and learning.

Example: Sophie enjoys playing with a set of kitchen toys. Instead of discussing them as "girly," her parent asks, "What do you like most about cooking with your toys?" Sophie explains that she loves creating new recipes and hosting pretend dinner parties, highlighting her creativity and social skills.

Why It Matters: This reflection encourages children to articulate their interests and preferences based on their experiences and enjoyment, rather than societal expectations. It promotes self-expression and helps children develop a sense of autonomy in their play choices.

➤ Model Breaking Gender Roles

How to Do It: As a parent, educator, or caregiver, actively model behaviour that challenges traditional gender norms. Play with toys associated with the opposite gender in front of children, demonstrating that toys are tools for imagination rather than symbols of gender.

Example: During family playtime, Ravi, a father, engages in playing with dolls alongside his daughter, showing that it's okay for boys to enjoy nurturing activities. Simultaneously, his daughter tries out building blocks, inspired by seeing her father's interest in creating structures.

Why It Matters: Modelling behaviour that breaks gender norms provides children with real-life examples of diverse interests and roles. It normalises a range of play activities and demonstrates that interests and activities are not confined by gender, fostering a more inclusive mindset.

➢ **Equal Play Opportunities**

How to Do It: Offer a variety of toys that encourage different skills and interests, ensuring that they are available to all children regardless of gender. Present these toys as valuable tools for everyone, emphasising their educational and developmental benefits.

Example: For a birthday party, a mix of toys is provided: construction sets, science kits, dolls, and art supplies. Each child is encouraged to explore and play with whatever piques their interest, ensuring that no toy is considered off-limits based on gender.

Why It Matters: Providing equal play opportunities helps dismantle the idea that certain toys are only for specific genders. It supports children in developing a diverse set of skills and interests, free from restrictive gender norms. This approach fosters a more balanced and inclusive view of play and learning.

A Final Thought: Unleashing Creativity Beyond Conventions

As we close this chapter on gendered toys, it's crucial to remember that this conversation extends beyond toys—it speaks to the core of how we envision and nurture each child's potential. The restrictive labels imposed by gendered toys can limit dreams and aspirations, but we have the power to redefine these boundaries.

Reflecting on the wisdom of the Bhagavad Gita, consider this verse:

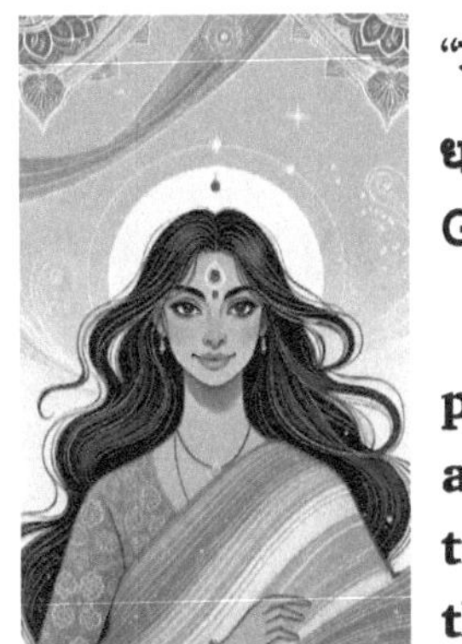

"उत्साहात्सहस्राणि योजयन्ति मनोऽभिः।

धनधान्यविवर्धन्ति प्रपन्ना बहुशः सदा॥ — Bhagavad Gita 6.34

"By practising enthusiasm and perseverance, one can achieve great heights and succeed in numerous endeavours, transcending the limitations imposed by the mind."

This shloka reminds us that true success and fulfilment come from within, not from external labels or constraints. It encourages us to cultivate enthusiasm and perseverance, qualities that empower us to transcend societal expectations and embrace our fullest potential.

Let's draw inspiration from figures like **Vikram Sarabhai** and **Kiran Mazumdar-Shaw** who defied conventional boundaries to pave new paths. Sarabhai's vision for India's space programme and Mazumdar-Shaw's success in biotechnology are testaments to the power of transcending limiting norms and embracing a broader vision.

Similarly, individuals like **Mr. Rajesh** who challenged the gendered constraints of toy marketing, and children like Anaya and Rohan who defied stereotypes, exemplify the impact of breaking free from outdated norms. Their efforts highlight how embracing a spectrum of possibilities can lead to greater inclusivity and creativity.

As we move forward, let us strive for a world where play and aspirations are guided by curiosity and passion, not constrained by gendered expectations. By fostering environments that support diverse interests and dreams, we honour the spirit of creativity and potential in every child.

Let's embrace this change and champion a future where every child's play is defined by their unique interests, unbounded by traditional labels.

In doing so, we contribute to a world where creativity and individuality are celebrated in all their forms.

Activity: "The Role Reversal Diary"

Objective: To challenge traditional gender norms by reflecting on and reimagining roles and interests through personal writing and introspection.

Materials Needed

➢ A journal or notebook.

➢ Pen or pencil.

➢ A quiet space for reflection.

Steps

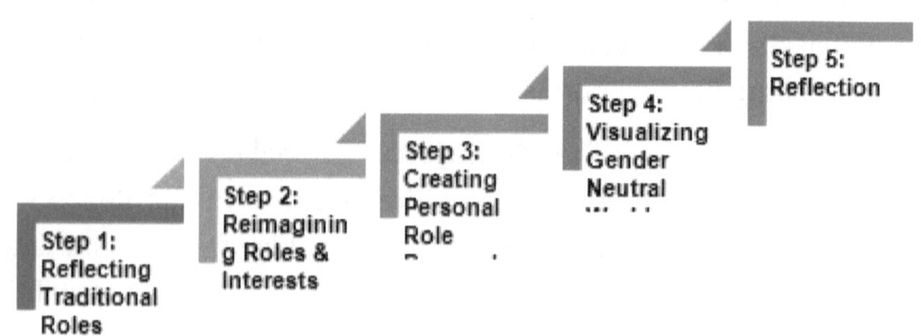

Step 1: Reflect on Traditional Roles

Begin by writing a brief reflection on how traditional gender roles have influenced your perception of interests and careers. Consider the roles and interests commonly associated with different genders in your culture or upbringing.

Example Prompt

> *"Reflect on a role or career traditionally*
> *associated with your gender."*
> *How did this influence your choices or interests*
> *growing up?*

Step 2: Reimagine Roles and Interests

Think about roles or careers that are traditionally gendered and imagine them in a gender-neutral context. Write a short description or story about a person who excels in a role typically associated with the opposite gender.

Example Prompt

> *"Write a story about someone who defies traditional*
> *gender roles. For instance, describe a male chef who is*
> *renowned for his pastry skills or a female engineer who*
> *pioneers in a male-dominated field. Focus on how their*
> *work and passion transcend gender expectations."*

Step 3: Create a Personal Role Reversal

Choose a role or interest that you've always felt drawn to but may have been discouraged from pursuing due to societal expectations. Write about how you would approach this role or interest if there were no gender constraints.

Example Prompt

Step 4: Visualise a Gender-Neutral World

Write a vision of a world where gender does not limit roles or interests. Describe how society, workplaces, and everyday life would look if everyone were free to pursue their passions without traditional constraints.

Example Prompt

Step 5: Reflect on Personal Insights

Conclude by reflecting on what you've learned through this activity. Consider how your perceptions of gender roles and interests have shifted. Write about any new insights or realisations you've had.

Example Prompt

Why This Matters

- ➤ **Encourages Self-Reflection:** This activity helps participants critically examine their own beliefs and experiences related to gender roles, fostering personal growth and awareness.

- ➤ **Promotes Gender Inclusivity:** By reimagining roles and interests, participants can challenge traditional norms and envision a more inclusive and equitable world.

- ➤ **Fosters Creativity:** The writing and reflection process encourages creative thinking and allows participants to explore new possibilities beyond societal constraints.

With warm reflection,

Sakhi

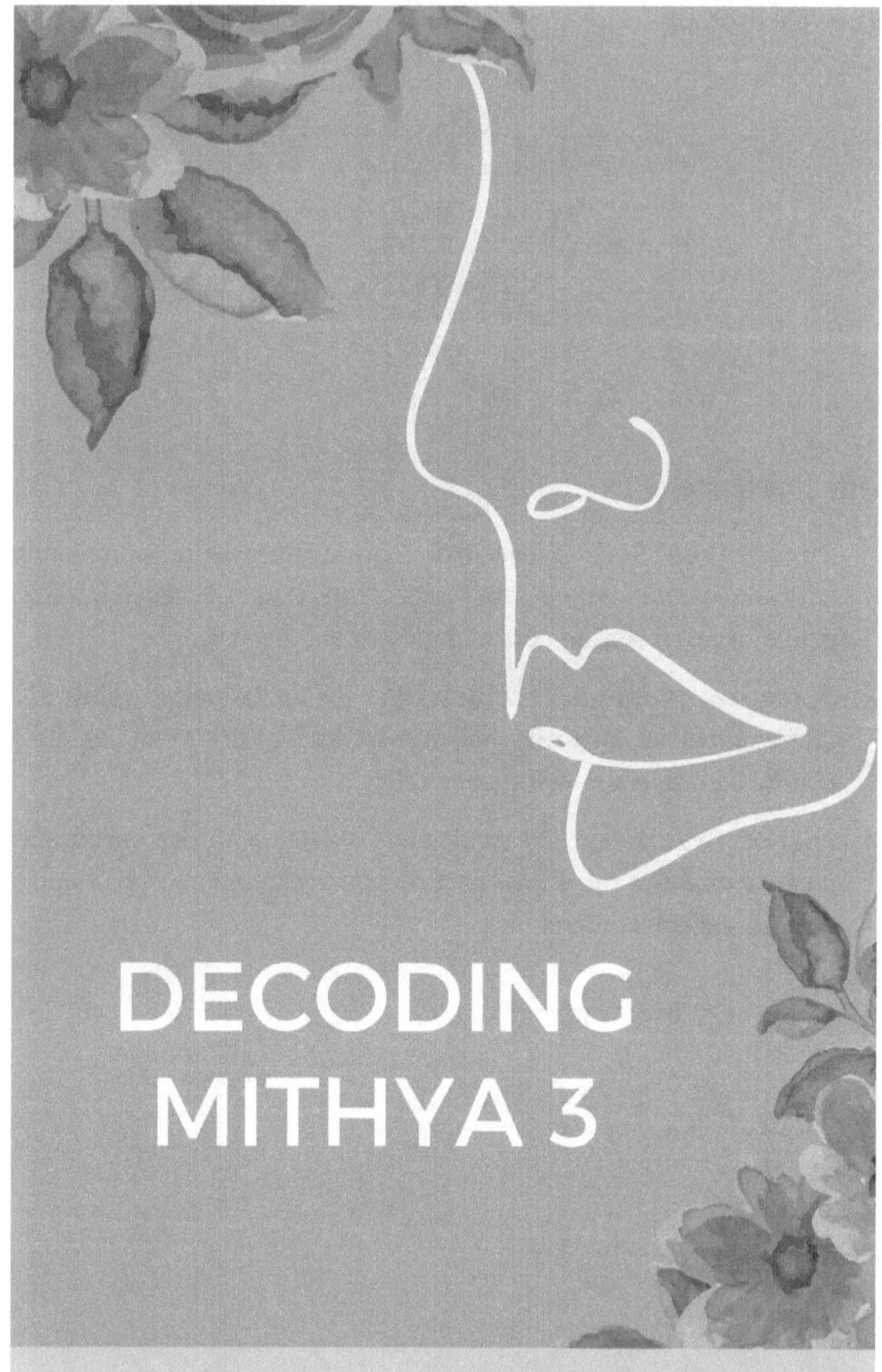
DECODING
MITHYA 3
FEMININE VS FEMINISM

Mithya 3
Feminine vs Feminism

The Silent War Within

> **The Famous 4: Decoding the Waves of Feminism**
>
> **To be Feminine or Being Feminist. The question being a women to being a empowered women**
>
> **Fighting the Odds of the Society over the ages**
>
> **Empowering the Women around you**

With each Mithya we break, we free ourselves a little more—unveiling the truth, shedding the weight of old beliefs, and stepping closer to a world of understanding and equality. The journey is not just about reflection, but transformation.

So, after breaking through Mithya 1 on colour stereotypes and Mithya 2 on gendered toys, I, Sakhi, am here again, holding up the mirror. Have you paused to reflect? To introspect?

Let's take a moment to ask ourselves some questions and see how far we've come:

1. When you see a young boy playing with dolls or a girl building with trucks, do you still feel the urge to guide them towards "gender-appropriate" toys?

2. Are you more conscious of how gendered labels might be influencing the decisions you make for children around you?

3. Have you found yourself questioning long-held beliefs about what colours, toys, or activities are "right" for boys and girls?

4. Do you support or feel more inclined to support brands and initiatives that promote gender-neutral choices for children?

Take a mental inventory. Each of these questions offers an opportunity to examine if those old patterns still linger within us. Change begins not just in our actions but in how we perceive the world around us.

We now journey into the intricate web of ***Feminine vs. Feminism.*** Let's dive into what it truly means to be a feminist.

Before We Dive In: Reflective Questions

1. Personal Definitions

- ✓ What does being "feminine" mean to you? Is it shaped more by personal choice or societal expectations?

- ✓ How do you define "feminism"? Is your understanding influenced by historical contexts, personal experiences, or contemporary movements?

2. Cultural and Societal Influences

- ✓ How have cultural or societal norms influenced your views on femininity? Reflect on specific messages or expectations you've encountered.

- ✓ In what ways have societal perceptions of feminism impacted your understanding or acceptance of feminist ideals?

3. Personal Alignment

- ✓ Do you feel that your personal values align more closely with traditional notions of femininity or with feminist principles? How so?

✓ Have you ever felt conflicted between upholding traditional gender roles and advocating for feminist principles? Share your experiences.

4. Influence of Role Models

✓ Who are the women or figures that have shaped your views on femininity and feminism? How have their actions or beliefs influenced your own perspective?

✓ What lessons have you learned from these role models about navigating the balance between feminine identity and feminist advocacy?

5. Experiences of Empowerment

✓ Can you identify moments in your life when you felt empowered by embracing feminist principles? What actions or events contributed to this sense of empowerment?

✓ Conversely, can you recall times when adhering to traditional femininity provided you with a sense of strength or identity? How did these experiences shape your view of empowerment?

6. Challenges and Misconceptions

✓ What challenges have you faced in reconciling feminist ideals with personal or societal expectations of femininity?

✓ What misconceptions about feminism have you encountered, and how have they affected your understanding of the movement?

7. Vision for Change

✓ How do you envision integrating feminist principles into your daily life? What changes or actions would support this integration?

✓ What impact do you hope to have on changing societal perceptions of femininity and feminism?

The Famous 4: Decoding the Waves of Feminism

As we sit with our reflections, turning over the stones of personal definitions and societal influences, let us embark on a journey through the intricate and often misunderstood terrain of feminism. This exploration is not merely an academic exercise; it is a quest to understand the multifaceted nature of feminism and its various waves, each of which has shaped our world in profound ways.

- **The First Wave: The Seeds of Change**

  - ✓ **Example:** Susan B. Anthony and Elizabeth Cady Stanton were pivotal figures in the First Wave of feminism. They championed the cause of women's suffrage in the United States, tirelessly advocating for women's right to vote. Their efforts culminated in the passage of the 19th Amendment to the U.S. Constitution in 1920, which granted women the right to vote.

  - ✓ **Impact on Society:** The First Wave laid the foundational stones for gender equality by challenging legal restrictions that denied women basic rights. It marked the beginning of organised efforts to address gender inequalities and set the stage for future feminist movements. By securing the right to vote, it empowered women to participate more fully in public life and politics, which had a ripple effect on other areas of societal reform.

- **The Second Wave: Expanding Horizons**

  - ✓ **Example:** Betty Friedan's seminal book, *The Feminine Mystique* (1963), ignited widespread discussion about women's roles in society. Friedan argued that the suburban ideal of the 1950s, which relegated women to domestic roles, was stifling their potential. Her work inspired many to question traditional gender roles and seek greater opportunities in the workforce and education.

  - ✓ **Impact on Society:** The Second Wave expanded the scope of feminist activism to address a wide array of issues, including workplace discrimination, reproductive rights, and gender roles. The establishment of Title IX in 1972, which prohibited discrimination based on sex in educational programmes and activities, was a direct result of Second Wave advocacy. This wave brought significant changes to laws and social attitudes, fostering greater gender equality in various aspects of life.

- **The Third Wave: Embracing Diversity**

  - ✓ **Example:** Audre Lorde, a prominent writer and activist, brought attention to the intersectionality of race, gender, and sexuality. Her work, such as *Sister Outsider* (1984), emphasised the need to address the diverse experiences of women from different backgrounds, challenging the predominantly white, middle-class perspective of earlier feminist movements.

  - ✓ **Impact on Society:** The Third Wave introduced a more inclusive approach to feminism, acknowledging that women's experiences are shaped by a complex interplay of factors such as race, class, and sexual orientation. This wave's focus on intersectionality led to a broader understanding of gender issues and promoted a more nuanced and inclusive feminist discourse. It also paved the way for greater recognition of the struggles faced by marginalised groups, leading to more inclusive policies and activism.

- **The Fourth Wave: Digital Empowerment**

  - ✓ **Example:** The #MeToo movement, initiated by Tarana Burke and popularised on social media, highlighted the pervasive issue of sexual harassment and assault. It provided a platform for individuals to share their experiences and advocate for systemic change. The movement quickly gained global traction, leading to significant cultural and legal shifts.

  - ✓ **Impact on Society:** The Fourth Wave harnessed the power of digital technology and social media to amplify feminist voices and mobilise global activism. It brought issues of sexual harassment and gender inequality to the forefront of public discourse, leading to increased awareness and calls for action. This wave's emphasis on intersectionality and global solidarity has led to ongoing efforts to address gender-based violence and inequality on a broader scale.

But now, my dear friends, let us turn our gaze inward and reflect on a question that often arises after such a historical exploration:

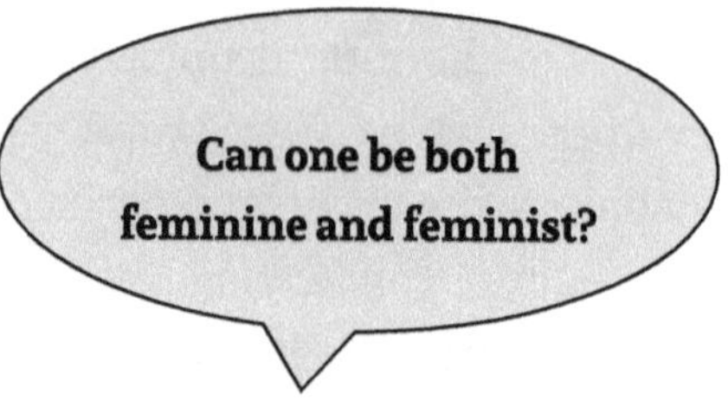

Society has long posed this as a paradox, but let us unravel this misconception together.

To Be Feminine or To Be Feminist?

Ah, the perennial dilemma—can one be both feminine and feminist? Society often creates a dichotomy, suggesting that to embrace one is to reject the other. But let us set the record straight: feminism does not demand that you choose between being feminine or feminist. Instead, it celebrates the ability to be both.

Understanding Feminine and Feminist

To be feminine is to embrace qualities traditionally associated with women—qualities such as nurturing, empathy, and grace. Society has long celebrated these attributes, often relegating them to the private sphere. But what if we reframe this perspective? What if femininity is not a limitation but a strength, a valuable facet of our identity that enriches our lives?

The Essence of Feminism

Feminism, on the other hand, is about challenging the status quo and advocating for equality. It is about ensuring that everyone—regardless of gender—has the freedom to choose their path without facing discrimination or limitation. Feminism is about recognising that every individual has the right to define their own identity and ambitions, unbounded by societal expectations.

The Harmony of Both

Let's consider an example to illustrate this harmony. Take the story of **Malala Yousafzai,** a young woman who has become a global symbol of resilience and empowerment. Malala's advocacy for girls' education and her stand against oppression embody the essence of feminism. Yet, her strength and leadership are also deeply connected to her cultural identity and personal experiences—elements of her femininity. She demonstrates that one can be both fiercely determined and profoundly compassionate, embodying both feminist ideals and feminine qualities.

Embracing Duality

The true power of feminism lies in its ability to accommodate and celebrate diverse expressions of identity. It does not ask us to conform to a singular notion of strength or softness. Rather, it invites us to be whole, to embrace all aspects of ourselves without shame or restriction.

A Call for Unity

But, my dear friends, let me remind you — to be feminist, you don't need to wage a war with men. Feminism doesn't seek division; it seeks unity. True feminism calls for men and women to stand together — not before or after, but as equals. That's where real change happens, when we walk side by side in this journey for equality.

The Path Forward

As we move forward in our journey towards equality, let us remember that the essence of feminism is choice and empowerment. It is about honouring each person's right to define their own identity and roles, free from societal constraints. So, whether you embody the nurturing qualities traditionally associated with femininity or the assertive traits often linked to feminist activism—or both—know that you are contributing to a world where everyone's voice matters, where everyone's choices are respected.

In this journey of embracing both femininity and feminism, we find a deeper understanding of ourselves and our place in the world. We learn that empowerment comes not from choosing sides but from harmonising the diverse aspects of our identities. So, let us walk this path with pride, knowing that being true to oneself—fully and unapologetically—is the ultimate expression of empowerment.

Ways to Change the Mindset for Mithya 3: Feminine vs. Feminism

1. "Reframe the Feminine" Daily Affirmations

- ➢ **Objective:** Redefine and celebrate feminine traits as powerful.

- ➢ **Method:** Every day, write or say out loud an affirmation that redefines a traditionally feminine trait in a positive and powerful way. For example:

  "My nurturing side is my strength, helping me build deep connections."

"Empathy is a superpower, not a weakness."

- ➢ **Impact:** This exercise helps internalise the idea that femininity is not at odds with feminism, but rather an integral part of being strong and self-assured.

2. Role Reversal Discussion: Feminine Strength

- ➢ **Objective:** Challenge conventional views on femininity by reversing roles.

- ➢ **Method:** In a group discussion or with a friend, switch the common **narrative.** For example, talk about how "soft skills" like empathy, care, and listening (often attributed to women) are key strengths in leadership. Likewise, discuss how feminism's emphasis on equality benefits everyone, not just women.

- ➢ **Impact:** This reversal forces participants to recognise the strengths that society often downplays, helping to break the mould of what feminism and femininity represent.

3. "Femininity in Action" Weekly Task

- ➢ **Objective:** Explore feminine traits in daily life and action.

- ➢ **Method:** Each week, choose a traditionally feminine trait (e.g., nurturing, cooperation, sensitivity) and consciously apply it to different aspects of your life—work, relationships, or community interactions. Notice how this impacts your sense of self and others' perceptions of you.

- ➢ **Impact:** This exercise emphasises the value of feminine qualities, reinforcing that they don't detract from feminist principles but enhance personal growth and collective empowerment.

4. "Feminism Without Labels" Social Media Challenge

- ➢ **Objective:** Normalise diverse expressions of feminism and femininity.

- ➢ **Method:** Use social media to showcase images, quotes, or stories that reflect both feminine qualities and feminist ideals. For example, a post about a nurturing woman who leads a successful company or a man embracing feminism. Create a hashtag like #FeminismWithoutLabels or #PowerOfFemininity to encourage others to participate.

> **Impact:** Publicly showcasing the overlap of feminism and femininity can help normalise the idea that both can co-exist harmoniously and expand the understanding of what feminism means.

5. Empathy Walk: Connecting Feminine & Feminist Perspectives

> **Objective:** Blend mindfulness with the exploration of gender dynamics.

> **Method:** Take a 15–30-minute walk in nature once a week. As you walk, reflect on the natural balance between nurturing and strength, mirroring how feminine and feminist qualities can co-exist. Consider how empathy, care, and leadership can blend and thrive together.

> **Impact:** This activity connects your reflection to nature, helping you internalise how seemingly opposing qualities can create balance and strength.

6. Gender Role Reversals in Daily Life

> **Objective:** Break traditional gender roles through behaviour.

> **Method:** For a day or a week, switch roles that society often associated with a specific gender. If you're typically seen as assertive, try showing more nurturing traits; if you're typically seen as nurturing, take a more assertive role. Reflect on how these changes make you feel and how others react.

> **Impact:** This experiment encourages you to explore how gender roles are social constructs and how embracing both femininity and feminism enhances personal and societal growth.

7. Reflective Journaling: Feminism and Femininity Coexistence

> **Objective:** Explore your personal understanding of feminism and femininity.

> **Method:** Spend 5-10 minutes journaling on how feminine traits (e.g., emotional intelligence, nurturing) have positively shaped your life and how feminism (e.g., equality, independence) has empowered you. Write about how these aspects complement each other, rather than conflict.

> **Impact:** This introspection helps you deconstruct rigid ideas about femininity and feminism, allowing for a broader, more inclusive mindset.

Final Thought: Together We Can Rise

A Thought from the Bhagavad Gita

As we contemplate the journey through Mithya 3, let us pause to reflect on a profound verse from the Bhagavad Gita:

"समं सर्वेषु भूतेषु तिष्ठन्तं परमेश्वरम्। (The Supreme Being exists equally in all beings.)

This ancient wisdom, spoken by Krishna to Arjuna, holds a timeless truth that resonates deeply with our exploration of feminism and gender equality. At its core, this shloka reveals a universal essence of equality, reminding us that despite the outward differences, every being shares an intrinsic, equal value.

The Real Meaning and Essence

In our modern world, where labels and societal expectations often seek to divide and diminish, this verse offers a sanctuary of equality. It serves as a reminder that the true essence of every individual transcends societal constructs. Whether you are a man or a woman, rich or poor, young or old, the divine essence within you remains untainted by external distinctions.

The essence of this teaching is that we are all equal in our intrinsic worth and our right to be heard, respected, and valued. It challenges us to rise above superficial distinctions and to recognise the inherent dignity and potential in every individual.

Final Thought: Together We Rise

As we close the chapter on Mithya 3, let this profound truth guide us forward. Feminism is not a battleground against men; rather, it is a call for unity and mutual respect. It invites us to join hands, to bridge divides, and to build a future where equality is not just an ideal but a lived reality.

The Real Power of Unity

Consider the example of Malala Yousafzai, whose advocacy for girls' education transcends gender. Her courage in speaking out was not against men but in partnership with allies of all genders who believed in her cause. Her journey illustrates how feminism—when embraced as a call for equality rather than division—can inspire global change.

Similarly, think of the men who have stood alongside women in the fight for gender equality. Figures like Patrick Stewart, who has been vocal about gender-based violence and the importance of women's rights, demonstrate that true feminism is about shared commitment to justice, not opposition.

Creating a Future of Equality

The essence of this unity lies in our daily interactions and choices. It is reflected in the way we challenge stereotypes, support each other's aspirations, and stand against injustice. By embracing the principle that we are all equal in our core essence, we can dismantle the barriers of inequality and build a more inclusive world.

The Path Forward

In our personal lives, let us strive to embody this equality. Support those around us in their pursuits, celebrate their achievements without prejudice, and advocate for a world where everyone, regardless of gender, can thrive as their true selves.

As we journey onward, let us remember that our strength lies in unity, in breaking down walls together, and in standing as equals. Together, we rise not by opposing each other but by embracing each other's potential and working towards a future where every person can live freely, authentically, and without constraint.

So, my dear friends, let us walk this path with conviction and grace. Let us champion the cause of equality and let our actions be a testament to the truth that at our core, we are all the same, deserving of respect, love, and opportunity.

In this spirit of unity and equality, may we find our strength and our purpose, and may we forge a world where every person can rise to their fullest potential.

Activity: Redefining Feminine and Feminist

Objective

To engage in self-reflection, challenge stereotypes about femininity and feminism, and explore how gender roles have shaped perceptions. This activity encourages participants/readers to redefine these concepts and understand their significance in their own lives.

Materials Needed

- A journal or blank paper
- Pens or markers

- Access to books, articles, or quotes about feminism (optional for further exploration)

- Comfortable space for reflection and writing

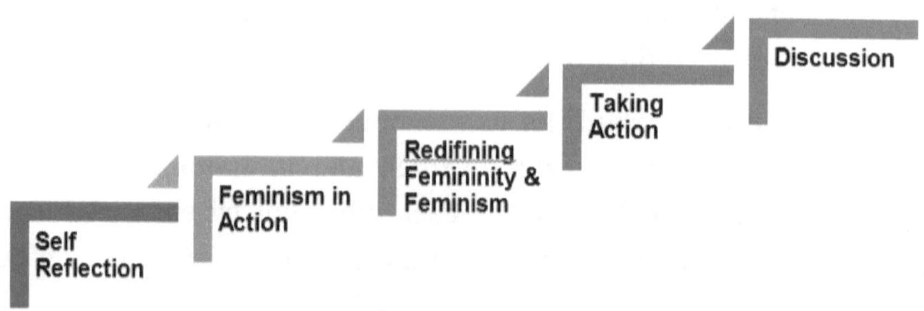

Step 1: Self-Reflection – Mapping Your Own Femininity

Activity

Take a few minutes to think about the qualities that are traditionally considered "feminine." Write these down on a piece of paper. Now, ask yourself these questions:

- Which of these qualities resonate with you personally?

- Have you ever felt pressured to embrace or reject certain feminine traits based on societal expectations?

- How do you define "feminine" for yourself?

Sakhi's Moment of Reflection

As I pause to consider what femininity means to me, I feel a quiet tension within. I cherish qualities like nurturing and empathy; they reflect my essence. But beauty? That's where doubt creeps in.

For so long, I thought I needed to conform to certain standards to be seen as feminine. Now, I wonder—must I?

I realise my worth isn't tied to my appearance. True femininity lies in embracing my authentic self, beyond the surface.

What about you? What qualities resonate with your own journey? Let's explore this together, redefining what it truly means to be feminine.

Step 2: Feminism in Action – Where Do You Stand?

Activity

Now, reflect on the concept of feminism. On another piece of paper, write down what feminism means to you. Then, think about:

- How has your understanding of feminism evolved over time?

- Have there been moments when you hesitated to identify as a feminist? Why?

- What actions do you take (or can take) in your daily life to support gender equality?

Sakhi's Reflection

I've often met people who hesitate to call themselves feminists, believing that feminism means rejecting femininity. But is that really the case?

Upon closer reflection, one might realise that feminism is not about abandoning softness or strength, but about championing choice and equality. It's about recognising that a woman has the right to embrace both vulnerability and resilience, just as a man has the right to be sensitive without judgement.

Feminism, at its core, is about freedom—the freedom to define ourselves beyond societal expectations, whether that means being soft, strong, or anything in between.

Step 3: Redefining Femininity and Feminism – Crafting Your Own Identity

Activity

On a new page, combine the insights from both reflections. Write a brief paragraph or statement that represents your own definition of femininity and feminism. This should be a personal manifesto that merges both concepts into one that feels true and empowering to you.

Sakhi's Reflection

"I am both feminine and feminist," someone might say, as they realise the 2 are not in conflict.

For them, being feminine means embracing their nurturing spirit, while being a feminist means standing for everyone's right to choose how they express themselves—free from the limits of gender roles. They recognise that empathy is a form of power, and true strength lies in unity and acceptance.

Feminism, then, is about empowering others to be their authentic selves, whether that self is soft, strong, or somewhere in between.

Step 4: Taking Action – Empowering Others

Activity

Now, reflect on the women (and men) in your life. Think of one person who has struggled with the expectations of femininity or feminism. Write down 3 ways you can empower them to embrace who they truly are, regardless of societal norms.

Sakhi's Reflection

You might find yourself supporting a friend who feels torn between her career and motherhood. In that moment, your empathy becomes her strength.

Perhaps you offer words of encouragement, reminding her that she's not alone. You might share stories of women who have successfully navigated both paths, or maybe you simply sit with her, listening without judgement, allowing her to express her fears and hopes.

Sometimes, being there—truly being present—is the greatest support we can offer, reminding her that her choices, whatever they may be, are valid and powerful.

Step 5: Discussion or Personal Reflection

Activity

After completing these steps, take a moment to reflect on the overall experience. If you're in a group, share your insights. If you're alone, write down your thoughts about the process. Reflect on these questions:

- How has this activity changed your view of femininity and feminism?

- Did you discover new perspectives on gender roles?

- What small changes can you make in your daily life to break down the barriers of femininity vs feminism?

Why This Matters

- Challenge Stereotypes: This activity pushes you to reconsider traditional notions of femininity and feminism, helping you embrace both without conflict.

- Empower Yourself: By redefining these terms on your own terms, you give yourself the power to navigate societal expectations with confidence.

- Support Others: This activity fosters empathy and action, encouraging you to uplift those around you in their own journeys of self-empowerment and equality.

With warm reflection,

Sakhi

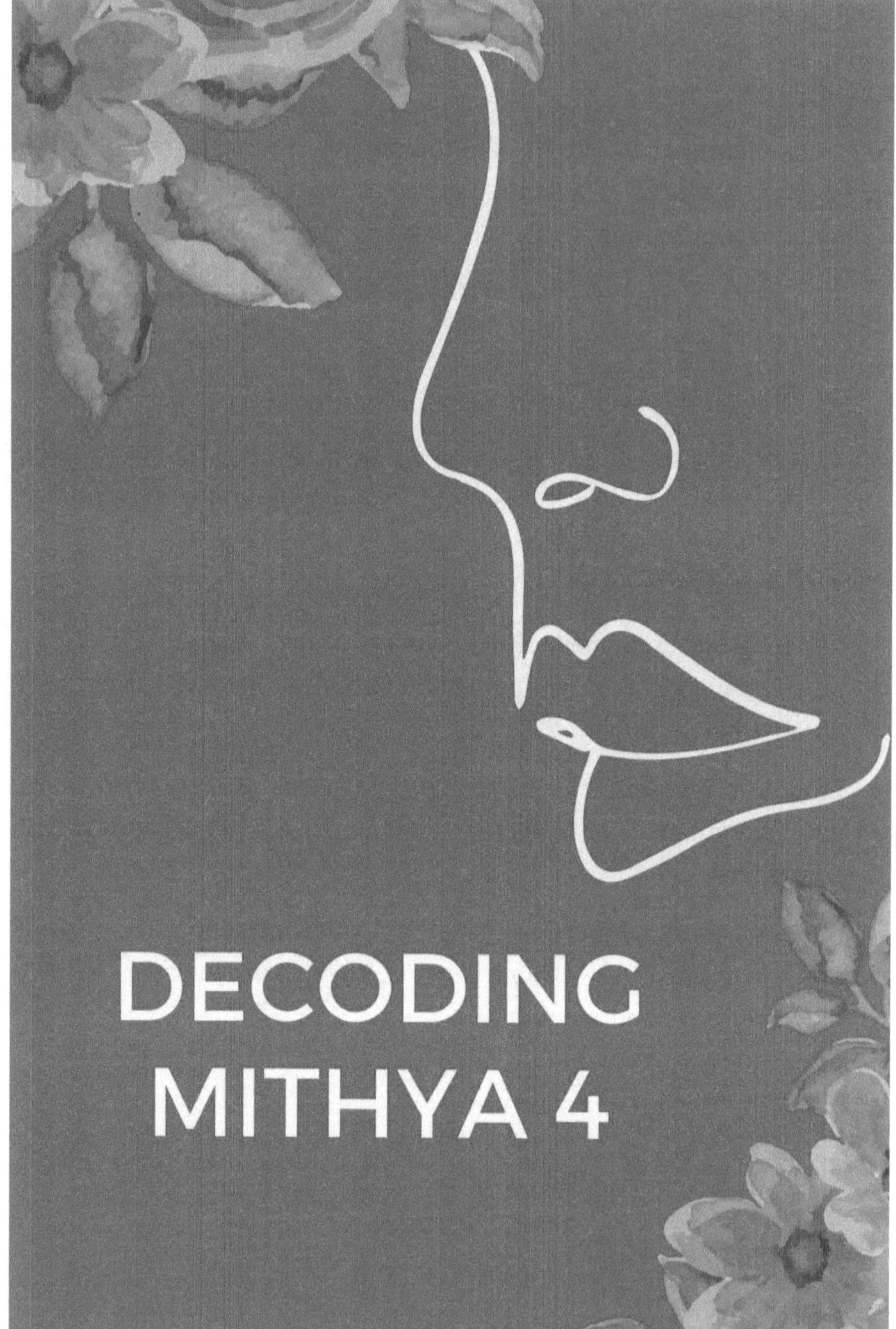

DECODING
MITHYA 4
MENSTRUATION TO MENOPAUSE

Mithya 4
Menstruation to Menopause

Breaking the RED Silence

Few Mithya's

Internalized Misogyny over the ages

Periods make women impure

Menopause means women are no longer attractive

Menopause causes madness

The secret to Women's Empowerment is WOMEN

Menstruation Time Tunnel 2 Happy to Bleed

Road to Happy Menopause

Learning to Unlearn Misogyny

With each Mithya we break, we free ourselves a little more—unveiling the truth, shedding the weight of old beliefs, and stepping closer to a world of understanding and equality. The journey is not just about reflection, but transformation.

Introspective Questions

- **Internal Reflection:** In the quiet moments of your day, have you ever paused to consider the beliefs you hold? Are there shadows of doubt that undermine your worth or that of other women? Reflect on how these thoughts ripple through your self-esteem and your relationships.

- **Historical Awareness:** As you journey through your understanding of menstruation and the roles women have played across generations, what echoes of the past resonate within you? Are there remnants of old beliefs that linger, shaping your present perceptions?

- **Cultural Influence:** Cultural traditions weave intricate patterns in our lives, often dictating how we view menstruation and gender roles. What practices or norms challenge your sense of modernity? In what ways do you find yourself caught between tradition and the values you hold dear?

- **Personal Impact:** Consider the silent, pervasive influence of internalised misogyny in your life. How has it shaped your interactions with other women? Reflect on the stereotypes that may have clouded your self-perception and the connections you form.

- **Future Vision:** Envision a future where misconceptions about menstruation and gender roles are dismantled. What steps can you take, however small, to foster change in your own life and within your community?

- **Menopause Awareness:** As the cycle of life continues, menopause emerges as a significant chapter. What beliefs or stereotypes have you encountered surrounding this transition? How have they coloured your understanding of ageing?

- **Emotional Experience:** In your circles, how comfortable are discussions about menopause? What feelings arise when you consider the openness—or lack thereof—around this phase of life?

- **Cultural Perspectives on Menopause:** Cultural narratives shape our perceptions profoundly. How do the attitudes towards menopause in your own background affect your feelings about ageing and femininity? Are there beliefs that seem ripe for re-evaluation?

- **Interpersonal Relationships:** Reflect on your connections with older women. How has your perception of menopause influenced these relationships? Is there a discomfort in discussing this natural transition, and if so, what lies at its heart?

- **Vision for Change:** Imagine the conversations that could flourish in a supportive environment regarding menopause. What role can you play in nurturing these dialogues? How might your contributions shift the narrative, creating a space of understanding and empowerment? 

As we reflect on these questions and uncover the layers of our own beliefs, let us turn our gaze inward to understand how these internalised notions of shame and competition shape our interactions and self-perceptions, particularly through the lens of internalised misogyny and its impact on our experiences with M – Menstruation & Menopause.

Internalised Misogyny and Menstruation: A Woven Tale

In a quaint village, young Riya grew up surrounded by whispers of disapproval every time she mentioned her menstrual cycle. Her mother, caught between tradition and modernity, was conflicted. On one hand, she taught Riya that menstruation was a natural process, a normal part of growing up that should be accepted with grace and understanding. Yet, despite this knowledge, her mother couldn't fully escape the clutches of old beliefs that labelled menstruation as a sign of impurity and secrecy.

In Riya's world, menstruation was cloaked in a veil of myth and shame. This societal discomfort with the natural menstrual cycle reflected a broader, pervasive misogyny. It wasn't just about the physical process; it was about the emotional and psychological impact of living in a world where a natural bodily function was wrapped in stigma and silence. This environment diminished Riya's self-worth and perpetuated her internal conflicts, leading her to navigate a landscape where she was expected to feel embarrassed or ashamed of something so fundamentally human.

Riya's experience is far from unique. Throughout history, women have grappled with internalised misogyny—a subtle yet powerful force that shapes how they view themselves and interact with others. Internalised misogyny manifests in various ways, often hidden beneath layers of social conditioning. For example, many women unconsciously adopt and perpetuate the same stereotypes and prejudices they have been subjected to, reinforcing the cycle of inequality.

One particularly troubling manifestation of this internalised misogyny is the phenomenon known as the "Pick-Me Girl." This term describes women who actively seek validation from men by positioning themselves as more agreeable, accommodating, or "one of the guys" compared to other women. They may undermine or criticise other women to gain favour or approval from men. This behaviour is deeply rooted in historical and societal conditioning that has long pitted women against each other.

The "Pick-Me Girl" phenomenon exemplifies how internalised misogyny operates on a subconscious level. It reflects the ingrained belief that a woman must differentiate herself from other women to be valued by men. This behaviour not only perpetuates division among women but also reinforces the patriarchal notion that female worth is contingent on male approval.

In Riya's context, this internalised misogyny extends beyond her own experiences to encompass a broader societal pattern. Women are often conditioned to view each other as competitors rather than allies, a dynamic that upholds the status quo of gender inequality. The secrecy and shame surrounding menstruation is just one example of how deeply ingrained misogynistic attitudes can influence and limit women's experiences and perceptions of themselves.

Understanding these dynamics is crucial for breaking free from the constraints of internalised misogyny. By acknowledging and addressing these ingrained biases, women can begin to dismantle the societal structures that perpetuate inequality and work towards a more equitable and supportive world.

Unravelling the Threads of Menstrual and Menopausal History: A Journey Through Time

The tale of menstruation and menopause in India is as ancient as the land itself, winding through millennia with a tapestry rich in both reverence and stigma. To understand the depth of the internalised misogyny surrounding these experiences, we must traverse through the ages, examining how attitudes have evolved and how they continue to shape our present.

Ancient India: A Sacred Process

In the Vedic Age (2000 BC – 500 BC), menstruation was not merely a biological event; it was an esteemed aspect of life. Ancient texts did not cast menstruating women as impure; instead, they recognised the menstrual cycle as a vital, natural rhythm of life. The Ambubachi Mela in Assam and Orissa serves as a vivid illustration of this reverence. This festival celebrates goddess Kamakhya's menstrual cycle, symbolising fertility and divine femininity. Rituals associated with this festival honoured the sacred nature of menstruation. It was a time when menstruation was perceived not as a mark of impurity but as a divine blessing, a celebration of life and creation.

Medieval India: The Shift Towards Superstition

As the centuries rolled on into the medieval period (7th – 16th century AD), the once-revered view of menstruation began to fracture under the weight of superstition and restriction. The emergence of beliefs that menstruating women could bring harm or attract malevolent spirits led to practices that isolated women from their communities during their cycles. In Kerala, the use of Onnara Mundu—special menstrual cloths—accompanied by strict taboos, symbolised this shift. Women were relegated to a state of seclusion, their cycles wrapped in secrecy and superstition, reflecting the societal anxieties of the time.

British Colonial Period: Introduction of Modern Products

The British colonial era introduced a new chapter in menstrual history with the advent of commercial menstrual products. In 1885, Southall's Sanitary Towels began making their way into Indian markets, marking a significant shift from traditional practices. However, despite this technological advancement, cultural stigmas continued to haunt menstruation. The arrival of modern products did not immediately dismantle the layers of secrecy and shame surrounding menstruation; rather, these products often coexisted with entrenched beliefs, leading to a complex interplay between innovation and tradition.

1980s – 1990s: Continued Secrecy and Superstition

The latter half of the 20th century saw significant strides in menstrual hygiene, with modern products becoming more widely available. Yet, in many parts of India, menstruation remained enshrouded in secrecy and superstition. Women frequently resorted to using rags or sand-filled garments, reflecting the deep-seated reluctance to openly discuss menstrual health. Traditional remedies and the minimisation of visible menstrual cloths were part of an ongoing effort to avoid reinforcing superstitions and stigmas.

Modern Era: Progress and Ongoing Challenges

The late 20th and early 21st centuries have brought about transformative changes in menstrual hygiene in India. Innovations like Arunachalam Muruganantham's low-cost sanitary pads addressed the critical issue of period poverty, making menstrual products more accessible to women in rural areas. Awareness campaigns spearheaded by NGOs and organisations have played a pivotal role in challenging long-standing taboos. Yet, despite these advances, significant challenges remain. In rural areas, women still face barriers to accessing modern menstrual hygiene products and often use unhygienic alternatives.

Menopause: The Unspoken Transition

As Riya transitioned into adulthood, she found herself not only grappling with the lingering stigma of menstruation but also facing the uncharted waters of menopause. This life stage, shrouded in silence and mystery, echoed many of the same societal anxieties that had characterised her experience with menstruation. Menopause, much like menstruation, was often viewed through a lens of shame, discomfort, and misunderstanding.

In a society that reveres youth, the onset of menopause can feel like a personal failure, a reminder of the inexorable passage of time. Women like Riya's mother often whispered among themselves, sharing tales of hot flashes and emotional upheaval, yet rarely speaking openly about their realities. This reticence perpetuated a cycle of silence, where menopause was seen as an ending rather than a natural transition in the continuum of life.

Historically, the perceptions of menopause have varied greatly. In some cultures, it was celebrated as a rite of passage, a time of wisdom and newfound freedom. However, in modern contexts, it is frequently met with discomfort and misconceptions, often reduced to a series of ailments rather than acknowledged as a significant life stage deserving of respect and understanding.

Cultural Dualism: Sacred vs. Impure

The historical journey of menstruation and menopause in India reveals a striking dualism: ancient practices that celebrated these processes as sacred juxtaposed against modern attitudes that often emphasise impurity and taboo. This cultural dualism underscores the urgent need for a shift in perception. Embracing the sacredness of menstruation and the wisdom of menopause, as understood in ancient times, while simultaneously addressing modern challenges and stigmas, is crucial for advancing women's health and equality.

The path forward involves harmonising cultural reverence with contemporary understanding, creating a space where both menstruation and menopause are recognised as natural and celebrated aspects of life, free from the constraints of outdated beliefs and practices. Only by unravelling these intertwined threads can we begin to weave a narrative that empowers women, fosters solidarity, and celebrates the full spectrum of the female experience.

Stories from Reality: Bridging the Gap

As I (Sakhi) stand here, once again holding a mirror to our beliefs, we uncover not only the myths of menstruation but also the stories that have shaped our understanding of menopause. These tales weave together the threads of history and culture, illuminating how practical needs and limited knowledge have morphed into enduring beliefs.

- **The Curious Case of Pickles**

Mithya: It was said that menstruating women could spoil pickles if they came into contact with them.

In the heart of a vibrant village, where pickles adorned every meal, this myth whispered its way through generations. Imagine young women, hesitant to enter the kitchen during their cycles, fearing the very essence of their womanhood would taint the cherished flavours. Yet, the truth is not so steeped in mystery.

Impact of Mithya: The myth instilled a sense of shame and exclusion, pushing women into the shadows of their own kitchens during a time when their contributions were vital.

Thoughtful Reflection: What lay behind this belief was a practical concern for hygiene. In a time when cloths were less absorbent and the art of sanitation was still taking shape, the risk of unclean hands touching the pickles sparked this age-old superstition. Today, with advanced hygiene practices, we see how such myths no longer hold ground, reminding us that often, what we fear is simply a reflection of our past ignorance.

- **The Bed Ban**

Mithya: Women were told to sleep on mats during menstruation to avoid staining mattresses.

Picture a modest home, where the wooden frames creaked under the weight of expectation. Here, the sanctity of a mattress was paramount. This belief was not born from notions of impurity, but rather from the desire to preserve what was precious.

Impact of Mithya: This restriction confined women to discomfort, perpetuating feelings of shame tied to their natural cycles.

Thoughtful Reflection: In times past, when menstrual products were rudimentary at best, women found practical solutions to manage potential leaks. The choice to sleep on mats was less about shame and more about practicality—a means to protect their belongings. As we embrace modern menstrual hygiene today, we can let go of such restrictions, freeing ourselves from the weight of outdated traditions.

- **The Kitchen Conundrum**

Mithya: It was believed that menstruating women should avoid cooking to prevent contaminating food.

Imagine the bustling kitchen, a space filled with laughter and the aroma of spices. Yet, amidst this vibrancy, women were often sidelined during their menstrual cycles. This exclusion stemmed not from true impurity but from a desire to ease their burden during a time when cooking demanded both physical strength and stamina.

Impact of Mithya: By sidelining women, this belief created a culture of exclusion that diminished their roles in the household and reinforced harmful stereotypes.

Thoughtful Reflection: As we reflect on this, we see that the practice was rooted in care, a misguided attempt to offer rest rather than reflect a belief in contamination. Today, as we embrace gender equality, let us also acknowledge the strength of women in kitchens, celebrating their roles rather than confining them to the shadows of tradition.

- **The Isolation Tradition**

Mithya: Menstruating women were often isolated from the rest of the household to prevent impurity.

Imagine a woman retreating to a quiet corner of the home, where solitude was expected rather than chosen. This isolation, initially a means of allowing women to rest during a physically demanding time, became cloaked in shame.

Impact of Mithya: This practice fostered feelings of loneliness and inadequacy, reinforcing the stigma that surrounds natural bodily functions.

Thoughtful Reflection: Historically, menstruation was linked to a period of rest due to the physically demanding tasks women performed. The isolation was a practical measure to ensure women could recuperate without additional physical strain. Over time, this practice became associated with impurity, even though its origins were rooted in practical health considerations. It is time to rewrite this narrative, integrating respect for tradition with a modern understanding of health and equality.

Menopause Myths: Bridging the Gap

Just as we have journeyed through the stories of menstruation, let us now delve into the narratives surrounding menopause, where myths intersect with reality.

- **The 'End of Womanhood' Myth**

Mithya: Menopause signifies the end of a woman's life and vitality.

In a society that often equates youth with worth, the arrival of menopause can feel like an unwelcome guest. Yet, let us reframe this notion.

Impact of Mithya: This belief can lead to feelings of loss and despair, making women feel diminished as they transition into this new phase.

Thoughtful Reflection: The transition is not an end but a new beginning, a time for rediscovery and empowerment. Women, as they step into this phase, often find themselves liberated from societal expectations, embracing new pursuits and passions. Menopause offers a chance to reflect on life's journey, celebrating experiences that define womanhood.

- **The Weight Gain Worry**

Mithya: All women gain significant weight during menopause due to hormonal changes.

Imagine a woman standing before the mirror, grappling with the number that seems to hold so much power over her self-image.

Impact of Mithya: This myth can create unnecessary anxiety, contributing to unhealthy body image issues and feelings of inadequacy.

Thoughtful Reflection: While hormonal shifts may influence weight, it is the choices we make—our diets, our activity levels—that truly shape our bodies. Let us challenge this narrative, empowering women to focus on health rather than fear, embracing their bodies in all their forms.

- **The Emotional Rollercoaster**

Mithya: Menopause leads to uncontrollable mood swings and emotional instability.

Envision a woman navigating the waves of her emotions, often portrayed as a caricature of instability.

Impact of Mithya: This stereotype diminishes the complexity of a woman's emotional landscape, framing her experiences as mere caricatures rather than recognising her depth.

Thoughtful Reflection: While hormonal changes can affect mood, it is essential to recognise the resilience that many women exhibit during this transition. Open dialogues about mental health can foster understanding and support, allowing women to embrace their emotions rather than fear them.

These stories illuminate how our past has shaped our present, revealing the complexities of both menstruation and menopause. By fostering open dialogue and integrating progressive practices with respect for historical context, we can challenge and deconstruct these myths. This journey is not merely about shedding old beliefs but about embracing a future where every phase of womanhood is celebrated and understood. Let us move forward together, weaving a narrative that honours both tradition and progress.

Transformative Actions: Breaking Free from Internalised Misogyny and Menstrual Taboos

As we embark on this journey of self-discovery and empowerment, let us uncover transformative actions that can guide us in breaking free from the shackles of internalised misogyny and the stigma surrounding menstruation and menopause.

- **Reflective Journaling**

Create a personal journal dedicated to exploring your experiences with internalised misogyny, menstrual taboos, and menopause. Begin by reflecting on specific instances where you may have reinforced or challenged these beliefs. Write about moments when societal expectations or personal biases influenced your actions or perceptions.

Sakhi's Reflection

I recall a moment when I discreetly tucked my menstrual products away, acutely aware of the judgement around me. That simple act reflected the shame society places on something so natural.

Similarly, in discussions about menopause, I hesitated to share my experiences, fearing misunderstanding. These moments reveal how societal expectations silence our truths.

Yet, in recognising these feelings, I feel a resolve to challenge these norms. By sharing our stories, we weave a tapestry of understanding, redefining what it means to embrace our bodies and affirm our experiences. Each voice matters, and together, we can dismantle the myths that confine us.

- **Empathy-Building Workshops**

Organise or attend workshops that facilitate open discussions about menstruation, menopause, and gender biases. Incorporate role-playing scenarios where participants share personal experiences and perspectives on topics like menstrual health and the emotional journey through menopause.

Sakhi's Reflection

Imagine a workshop where participants engage in role-playing. One might express the burden of menstrual stigma, while another shares how menopause signifies a new beginning. This exchange opens a window into our shared experiences, revealing the layers of societal attitudes that shape our perceptions.

Following these role-plays, a group discussion can deepen this exploration. By sharing our diverse stories, we cultivate empathy and challenge the preconceived notions surrounding menstruation, menopause, and gender biases. In this dialogue, we not only find common ground but also foster understanding, empowering each other to redefine our narratives.

- **Support Networks**

Form or join a peer support group focused on menstrual health, menopause, and combating sexism. Use this space to share personal stories, offer mutual support, and develop strategies for addressing and challenging biases.

Sakhi's Reflection

Imagine a monthly support group gathering, where individuals come together to share their experiences with menstrual taboos, menopause, and internalised misogyny. In this safe space, members recount personal stories, offering each other support as they confront societal stigmas. Together, they brainstorm community outreach activities aimed at raising awareness.

The goal is to foster an environment of openness where discussions dismantle the stigmas surrounding menstruation and menopause. Through these shared experiences, the group strengthens community ties and inspires collective action against gender biases, empowering each member to embrace their journey.

- **Educational Campaigns**

Develop or participate in community education initiatives aimed at addressing menstruation, menopause, and gender stereotypes. Use creative formats like social media campaigns, informative videos, and public talks to disseminate accurate information and challenge misinformation.

Sakhi's Reflection

Picture a vibrant social media campaign, alive with short, engaging videos that dispel common myths about menstruation and menopause. Each clip, infused with humour and clarity, educates viewers while inviting them to join the conversation.

Complementing this digital outreach, imagine a public talk or workshop where experts and advocates gather to share their insights on menstrual health and menopause. The atmosphere buzzes with curiosity as questions are answered and knowledge is exchanged.

The goal is clear: to raise awareness and challenge misinformation through engaging and educational initiatives. By empowering individuals with accurate information, we foster a more informed and inclusive community, breaking down the barriers of silence and stigma.

- **Self-Acceptance Practices**

Implement daily practices that promote self-acceptance and challenge self-deprecating thoughts. Engage in activities such as affirmations, meditation focused on self-compassion, and setting personal goals that defy traditional gender norms.

Sakhi's Reflection

Begin each day with affirmations that honour your unique strengths, gently challenging any negative self-beliefs that arise. Embrace a meditation practice centred on self-compassion, visualising yourself fully embracing your authentic self through every phase of womanhood.

Set personal goals that defy traditional gender expectations—whether it's pursuing a career that inspires you or sharing your menopause journey to empower others. Each step you take is a testament to your courage and individuality.

Cultivate a positive self-image and diminish internalised misogyny by fostering self-acceptance. Challenge limiting beliefs and affirm your worth, proving that your capabilities transcend conventional gender stereotypes.

Addressing Menopause: Transformative Practices

As we continue this exploration, it's crucial to integrate practices specifically focused on the menopause journey, honouring the richness of this phase in a woman's life.

- **Celebratory Gatherings**

Host or participate in gatherings that celebrate the transition of menopause. These spaces can be filled with shared stories, laughter, and collective wisdom, breaking the silence that often surrounds this life stage.

Sakhi's Reflection

Picture a circle of women, each sharing their unique experiences with menopause: hot flashes, mood swings, and moments of unexpected freedom. Through storytelling, laughter, and heartfelt solidarity, these gatherings shift the narrative from one of loss to one of empowerment and growth.

Cultivate a strong sense of community among women, creating a space where menopause is celebrated as a transformative stage of life, free from stigma and shame.

- **Mindfulness and Movement**

Engage in mindfulness practices and physical activities that honour your body and its changes. Yoga, tai chi, or even simple walks in nature can serve as reminders to listen to your body and nurture it during this transition.

Sakhi's Reflection

Imagine joining a yoga class designed specifically for women in menopause, where every pose honours the strength and wisdom of your body. As you move and breathe, you discover ways to celebrate this journey of transformation.

Deepen your connection with your body, fostering acceptance and well-being as you embrace the changes that menopause brings.

These transformative actions not only light the way for us to break free from the chains of internalised misogyny and the stigma surrounding menstruation, but they also honour the richness of every woman's journey, including the profound transition of menopause. By embracing these practices, we reshape narratives and cultivate empathy, forging a more inclusive world where each phase of womanhood is celebrated and understood. Together, let us weave a tapestry of resilience and empowerment, creating spaces where every voice is heard, valued, and uplifted.

Bhagavad Gita Insight

In the timeless wisdom of the Bhagavad Gita, Lord Krishna imparts a profound lesson through the shloka:

"Karmaṇy-evādhikāras te mā phaleṣhu kadāchana | Mā karma phala hetur bhūr mā te saṅgo 'stv akarmaṇi ||"

(Chapter 2, Verse 47)

This verse reminds us: you have the right to perform your duties, but you are not entitled to the fruits of your actions. It urges us to focus on our actions, unburdened by attachment to the outcomes. In our quest to dismantle internalised misogyny and menstrual taboos, it calls us to act with integrity, unshackled from societal expectations and personal biases.

Final Thought

As we navigate the intricate web of internalised misogyny and the stigmas surrounding menstruation, we unearth a profound truth: true transformation begins within each of us. It is through confronting and dismantling deeply ingrained beliefs, embracing our authentic selves, and nurturing empathy that we lay the groundwork for a more just and enlightened world.

Consider the journey of Riya, a woman who grew up in a village shrouded in the secrecy and shame of menstruation. Her story encapsulates the struggle many women face—not just against societal taboos, but against the internalised messages that whisper their natural processes are something to be hidden. Riya's path toward self-acceptance and advocacy illuminates the personal transformation possible when we dare to challenge these myths.

Then there's Lakshmi from Tamil Nadu, who bravely questioned the traditional ban on menstruating women entering the kitchen. Her journey reveals how understanding the origins of such practices can lead to inclusive and practical solutions. By recognising that these restrictions often stemmed from outdated concerns, she advocated for a balanced approach that respects both tradition and modern sensibilities.

Reflective journaling becomes a vital tool in this transformative process. As we put pen to paper, we gain deeper insights into our biases and societal influences. This practice allows us to acknowledge our internalised beliefs while guiding us to challenge and reshape them.

Empathy-building workshops, where participants share their personal experiences, serve as powerful conduits for understanding. By stepping into one another's shoes, we learn to appreciate the diverse narratives that shape our lives, fostering a collaborative spirit in dismantling stigmas and promoting inclusivity.

Support networks, where individuals gather to discuss menstrual health and gender biases, create nurturing spaces for mutual support and collective action. These groups cultivate solidarity, reinforcing the shared purpose of challenging societal norms.

Moreover, educational campaigns that disseminate accurate information about menstruation and gender stereotypes play a crucial role in raising awareness. Through creative and engaging formats, we can combat misinformation and nurture a more informed and inclusive community.

Lastly, self-acceptance practices—like affirmations and meditation—empower us to embrace our true selves. By celebrating our strengths and pursuing goals that defy traditional gender norms, we assert our worth and capabilities beyond societal expectations.

Each step we take toward understanding, respect, and empathy transforms not only our individual lives but also contributes to a larger movement toward equality. As we confront and dismantle these myths, we create a ripple effect, fostering a culture of respect and empowerment for all.

I, Sakhi, invite you to reflect deeply on the lessons we've explored today. Let us face these myths with courage and clarity, breaking free from the constraints that bind us. Each act of understanding and respect we undertake contributes to a collective journey towards equality and justice.

May we embark on this journey with renewed resolve and steadfast commitment to making a difference. Together, let us forge a path towards genuine respect, empowerment, and equality for everyone.

Activity: Breaking the Chains of Misogyny and Menstrual Stigmas

Objective: To confront internalised misogyny and menstrual taboos through creative reflection and collective action, fostering awareness and empowerment.

Materials Needed

- Art supplies (paper, markers, crayons, clay).

- Journals or notebooks.

- Role-play props (simple costumes, everyday objects).

- Access to the internet or printouts for research.

- A comfortable space for group discussion.

Activity & Steps

- Myth-Busting Through Art

Activity: Create a visual representation of a common menstrual or misogynistic myth and its underlying truth.

Step 1: Use art supplies to draw or sculpt an image that depicts a common myth about menstruation or internalised misogyny. For example, illustrate the myth that menstruation is impure by showing how this belief can manifest in everyday life.

Step 2: Next to your artwork, write a brief explanation of the real, factual information that dispels the myth. For instance, depict a scene where menstruation is celebrated or accepted, countering the notion of impurity.

Sakhi's Reflection

Creativity becomes a vital means to challenge the myths that cloud our understanding of womanhood. Through art, we can visualise the complexities of experiences like menstruation, transforming societal misconceptions into powerful statements. Each brushstroke or word crafted is an invitation to see beyond the surface, to engage in deeper conversations about our truths.

As we express ourselves, we not only reclaim our narratives but also encourage others to reflect on their own beliefs. This creative journey allows us to unravel the layers of misunderstanding, celebrating the richness of our stories. In doing so, we foster empathy and understanding, paving the way for a more inclusive narrative that honours every woman's unique journey.

- **Role-Playing Realities**

Activity: Engage in role-playing scenarios to experience and address internalised misogyny and menstrual stigmas.

Step 1: Divide participants into small groups. Assign each group a scenario related to menstrual taboos or internalised misogyny (e.g., a woman facing workplace discrimination due to menstruation or a "Pick-Me Girl" undermining other women).

Step 2: Each group role-plays their scenario, focusing on how the characters might confront and resolve the situation. Use props and costumes to enhance the role-playing experience.

Step 3: After each role-play, discuss the scenarios as a group. Reflect on what was learned and how these insights can be applied to real-life situations.

Sakhi's Reflection: In the quiet act of creation, we uncover the strength to confront the myths that shape our experiences. Picture the gentle brushstrokes or the cadence of poetry revealing the intricate layers of womanhood, from menstruation to menopause. Each piece becomes a mirror, inviting reflection and dialogue.

As we share our stories—vulnerable and authentic—we dismantle the stigma that binds us, transforming individual narratives into a powerful collective voice. This journey fosters empathy and honours the rich tapestry of women's experiences, paving the way for a more inclusive world where every voice resonates and is valued.

- **Reflective Journaling**

Activity: Document personal reflections on experiences with internalised misogyny and menstrual taboos.

Step 1: Set aside time for journaling. Write about specific moments when you've encountered or perpetuated menstrual or misogynistic myths. Reflect on how these experiences have affected you and others.

Step 2: Include prompts such as: "When have I felt limited by gender expectations?" or "How have I challenged or reinforced menstrual taboos in my life?"

Sakhi's Reflection: Reflective journaling invites us to explore our experiences with internalised misogyny and menstrual taboos. By documenting moments when we felt constrained by gender expectations or silent about our bodies, we create a space for self-discovery.

Prompts like ***"When have I felt limited?"*** help us uncover biases and recognise patterns in our behaviour. This process not only enhances our self-awareness but also guides us towards growth and empowerment. Through our reflections, we forge a narrative of resilience, paving the way for a future where every woman's voice is valued and celebrated.

Empathy-Building Dialogue

Activity: Facilitate a group discussion focused on sharing experiences and fostering empathy.

Step 1: Gather participants and initiate a discussion about personal experiences with menstrual health and gender biases. Encourage open sharing and active listening.

Step 2: Use guided questions like: "How have societal expectations around menstruation impacted your view of yourself?" or "In what ways have you seen internalised misogyny play out in daily life?"

Sakhi's Reflection: In the sacred space of dialogue, we discover the profound power of shared experiences. As we gather to discuss our journeys with menstrual health and gender biases, each voice adds a unique thread to the tapestry of understanding. Through open sharing and active listening, we foster a culture of empathy that transcends individual stories.

Guided by thoughtful questions, we delve into how societal expectations shape our self-perceptions and reveal the subtle ways internalised misogyny manifests in our lives. This collective reflection not only nurtures mutual support but also creates a safe haven for challenging stigmas. In this nurturing environment, we empower one another, paving the way for deeper connections and a more inclusive narrative that honours the diverse realities of all women.

- **Community Education Campaign**

Activity: Develop a mini-campaign to educate others about menstrual health and gender biases.

Step 1: Choose a format for the campaign (e.g., a social media post, flyer, or community presentation). Create content that addresses common myths and provides factual information.

Step 2: Include personal stories, visual elements, and actionable steps for readers to challenge stigmas and advocate for change.

Sakhi's Reflection: In the spirit of community, we find the strength to challenge the myths that cloud our understanding of menstrual health and gender biases. By developing a mini-campaign, we transform our knowledge into action, crafting messages that resonate and educate. Whether through vibrant social media posts, informative flyers, or engaging presentations, each piece of content becomes a beacon of truth.

Incorporating personal stories and visual elements allows us to connect on a deeper level, making our campaign not just informative but also relatable. By providing actionable steps, we empower others to join this vital movement, encouraging them to confront stigmas and advocate for change. Together, we cultivate a culture of awareness and respect, paving the way for a future where every voice is heard and every experience is valued. In this shared journey, we celebrate our collective strength and the beauty of diverse narratives.

Closing Reflection

As we gather our thoughts, I invite each of you to share the insights and experiences that have emerged from our time together. These hands-on activities have not merely served as exercises; they have been gateways to understanding, opening our eyes to the deep-seated biases that often go unexamined.

In sharing our stories and engaging in dialogue, we have begun to dismantle the internalised misogyny and menstrual taboos that shape our perceptions. Each of us has confronted the narratives that confine us, transforming them into pathways for growth and understanding. It is in this shared space that we find strength—strength to challenge the status quo, to voice our truths, and to advocate for change.

Let us carry forward this momentum, committing to ongoing reflection and action in our daily lives. By continuing to confront these barriers, we not only empower ourselves but also inspire those around us to do the same. Together, we can cultivate a more inclusive and respectful society, one where every woman's journey is honoured, and every voice is valued. In this tapestry of shared experience, we find the threads of resilience and hope, weaving a brighter future for all.

With warm reflection,

Sakhi

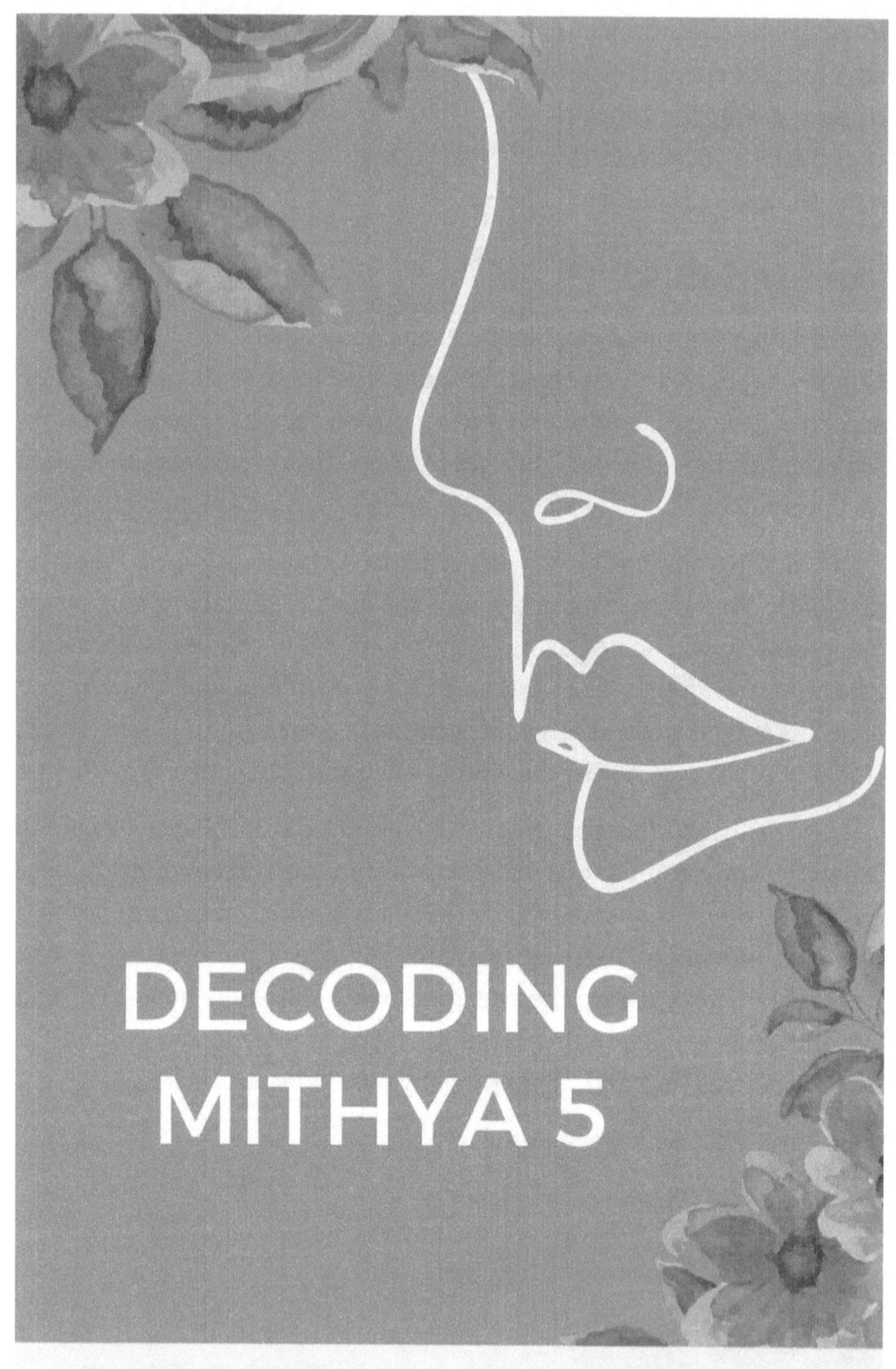

DECODING MITHYA 5

Mithya 5
Financial Literacy

Beyond the Myths: A Pathway to Financial Empowerment

Mithya's

Investment is too risky for women

Women can't handle complex financial products

Women don't earn as much because they don't negotiate salaries

Gender Pay Gap

Decoding Mithya

Financial Independence

Busting the Myth Pink Tax

Financial Freedom 2 Financial Literacy

Financial Independence vs. Financial Freedom: This Key Difference Changes Everything...

In the bustle of everyday life, we often celebrate women's achievements and their growing presence in various fields. Yet, amid these triumphs, a question lingers: While women are increasingly earning, how many are truly empowered to manage, save, and invest their earnings? How many are actively involved in financial decisions, from paying income tax to strategising investments? Why do financial decisions often rest with fathers, husbands, or sons, even when the women themselves are earning and contributing?

I am Sakhi, here to break the myth surrounding financial illiteracy—a myth that persists despite the advancements women have made in various domains. The COVID-19 pandemic presented a stark illustration of this issue. Many women found themselves in a heart-wrenching situation, suddenly facing financial uncertainty after losing their spouses, with little to no understanding of their family's finances. These real-life stories underscore a critical reality: financial literacy among women remains a significant challenge, deeply rooted in societal norms and gender biases.

Reflective Questions

➤ How prepared are you for financial emergencies?

➤ When was the last time you reviewed your financial goals and strategies?

➤ Do you feel confident discussing financial matters or making investment decisions?

These questions are more than mere reflections; they are invitations to examine and challenge the norms that have perpetuated financial illiteracy among women. Financial literacy is not just about understanding numbers – it's about gaining control, confidence, and the ability to make informed decisions that can profoundly impact one's life.

The Illusion of Financial Independence

Take Misha, for instance. Misha's high-paying job and apparent financial success masked a deeper struggle. Despite her impressive income, she felt a constant unease due to her limited financial knowledge and dependence on her brother for financial advice. This dichotomy—between visible success and internal insecurity—highlights a common misconception: financial independence is often mistaken for financial freedom.

Financial independence typically refers to having enough assets or income to cover one's expenses without the need to work. It's a numerical goal that can seem elusive and requires disciplined saving and investing. However, true financial independence is not merely about reaching a number; it's about feeling secure and self-empowered.

On the other hand, financial freedom is a mindset. It's not about a specific figure but about a state where money no longer dictates your choices. It's about aligning your spending with your core values and valuing experiences over mere cost. Financial freedom can be achieved long before reaching the pinnacle of financial independence.

The Pink Tax: A Gendered Pricing Dilemma

As I reflect on Aisha's frustration while shopping for razors, I can't help but empathise with her disbelief. In her quest for a simple grooming tool, she found 2 nearly identical products—one cloaked in pink, the other in blue. Yet, the pink razor bore a price tag that was significantly higher. This moment wasn't just an annoyance; it was a clear illustration of the pink tax—a gender-discriminatory pricing practice that many women encounter daily.

The pink tax, though not an official tax, reveals the deep-seated gender biases embedded in our consumer culture. Research from the New York City Department of Consumer Affairs exposes a troubling reality: women often pay up to 43% more for similar hygiene products than men. This disparity doesn't just burden women financially; it reinforces damaging stereotypes that suggest women's needs are less worthy of consideration, thus perpetuating a cycle of inequality.

In Canada, the situation is similarly alarming. Women have found themselves paying over 50% more for unisex hygiene products compared to their male counterparts. As I hear the stories of women like Aisha, I am reminded that this issue is not merely statistical—it is personal, affecting the lives of countless women who work hard for every rupee they earn.

Turning our gaze to India, I recall Neha, a young professional navigating the bustling markets of Mumbai. One day, she discovered that her favourite brand of shampoo, marketed specifically for women, was priced much higher than the equivalent product for men. When she inquired at the store, the sales clerk casually remarked, "That's just how it is; women's products are always pricier." Neha felt a mix of frustration and resignation, realising that this was not an isolated incident but part of a broader trend that devalued her choices.

Then there's Gauri, a college student in Delhi, who faced similar challenges while shopping for personal care items. She often found herself standing in front of shelves lined with pink packages, each one whispering promises of beauty and elegance, yet demanding a higher price. Gauri's friends laughed off the disparity, saying, "It's just how the world works," but Gauri was determined to challenge that narrative. She began sharing her experiences on social media, igniting conversations about gendered pricing and sparking awareness among her peers.

These stories, echoing across cities and communities, highlight the insidious nature of the pink tax. Despite legislative efforts like the "Pink Tax Repeal Act" in the U.S., significant changes remain elusive.

> Why do we accept this disparity?
> What message does it send to our daughters and sisters when they see products marketed to them priced higher than those for men?
> Are we truly okay with being charged more simply because of our gender?

The pink tax is more than just a financial burden; it is a call to action. As we share our stories and lift our voices, we pave the way for a more equitable future, where products are priced fairly, regardless of gender. Together, we can dismantle these outdated notions and strive for a world where all women's choices are valued, not penalised.

Are we ready to stand together and make this change?

As we delve deeper into the conversation about the pink tax and its implications, I find myself reflecting on another crucial aspect of empowerment: financial literacy. In a world where pricing disparities persist, understanding the intricacies of financial management becomes essential for women seeking to reclaim their autonomy.

Financial Literacy: Empowering Women Through Knowledge

This question resonates deeply, connecting us to a crucial aspect of addressing ***Gender Inequities: Financial Literacy.*** To illustrate this, let me share a poignant story.

Take the case of Deepa, who, after the sudden loss of her husband to suicide, found herself not only grieving but also grappling with the harsh reality of her financial situation. She was left with little understanding of their financial assets, bills, or investments—details that had been solely managed by her husband. In the aftermath, as she sifted through papers and accounts, she realised how unprepared she was to take charge of her family's financial future.

During the COVID-19 pandemic, countless women faced similar challenges. With many husbands falling victim to the virus, families were left behind without a clear understanding of their finances. Wives, daughters, and mothers were thrust into the role of financial decision-makers overnight, often without the necessary knowledge or tools to navigate the complexities of managing money.

Moreover, the pervasive issue of the gender pay gap further complicates women's financial realities. Take the story of Meera, a talented software engineer who discovered she was earning significantly less than her male counterparts for the same role. Despite her qualifications and contributions, the disparity left her feeling undervalued and frustrated. Meera's experience is not unique; many women face similar challenges, leading to long-term financial consequences that can affect their ability to save, invest, and plan for the future.

How can we ensure that no woman faces such uncertainty again?

What if we empowered each woman with the knowledge to manage her finances, to understand investments, savings, and budgeting?

Wouldn't that be a way to dismantle not just the pink tax, but all forms of financial inequality?

By prioritising financial literacy, we can equip women with the skills they need to take control of their finances. We can teach them to recognise unfair pricing practices and advocate for themselves in the marketplace. Empowering women through knowledge not only enables them to make informed decisions but also fosters a sense of independence and confidence.

Together, we can challenge outdated notions, support one another, and create a community where every woman has the tools to thrive financially. As we lift our voices and share our stories, we pave the way for a future where financial literacy becomes a cornerstone of women's empowerment—helping to ensure that no one is left unprepared, regardless of the challenges they face.

Breaking the Myths: Practical Exercises to Foster Financial Empowerment

> **Budgeting Exercise:** Develop a detailed monthly budget. Track your income and expenses, categorise your spending, and identify areas for potential savings. This practice enhances your understanding and control over your finances.

> **Financial Goals Worksheet:** Define both short-term and long-term financial goals. Clarify what financial independence and freedom mean to you personally. Break these goals into actionable steps and set timelines for achieving them.

> **Pink Tax Awareness:** Compare prices of similar products marketed towards different genders. Document your findings and consider supporting brands that practice gender-neutral pricing. Use this knowledge to raise awareness about the pink tax.

> **Investment Education:** Spend an hour each week learning about different types of investments (stocks, bonds, mutual funds, etc.). Utilise online courses, webinars, or financial blogs to build your investment knowledge and confidence.

> **Mindset Reflection:** Reflect on your financial mindset. Are your decisions driven by price alone, or do you consider value and cost? Practice shifting your focus from price to value in your financial decisions.

Bhagavad Gita Shloka

"यथा दीपो निवातस्थो नेङ्गते सोपमायथा।

योगिनो यतचित्तस्य युञ्जतो योगमात्मनः॥"

— भगवद्गीता 6.19

"When meditation is mastered, the mind is unwavering like the flame of a lamp in a windless place."
– Bhagavad Gita 6.19

This shloka emphasises the importance of clarity and control. Just as a steady flame remains undisturbed in a still environment, our financial decisions can remain stable and purposeful when guided by knowledge and self-awareness.

Final Thought

As we navigate this mithya, let's embrace the journey toward financial empowerment. Financial freedom is not a distant destination but a continuous journey—a state where money aligns with our values and does not dictate our decisions. Embrace financial literacy not merely as a tool for independence but as a pathway to a fulfilling and purposeful life. By challenging and dismantling the myths surrounding financial illiteracy, we can pave the way for a future where financial empowerment is a reality for all.

Consider Deepa, who transformed her life by seeking knowledge and understanding after her husband's passing. She learned to manage her finances, investing in her education and starting a small business that not only supported her family but also empowered other women in her community. Through workshops and mentorship, she shared her story, inspiring others to break free from the cycle of dependence and financial ignorance.

Similarly, Meera, after advocating for herself and others at her workplace, became a champion for pay equity. She organised discussions, gathered data, and approached management with compelling arguments for equal pay. Her efforts led to significant changes within her organisation, not only benefiting her but also creating a more equitable workplace for all women.

These stories remind us that financial empowerment is not just about personal gain; it's about lifting others along the way and challenging systemic barriers. As we conclude this Mithya's, let us carry the stories of these remarkable women with us, using them as beacons of hope and inspiration.

It's not just about achieving financial independence for ourselves; it's about creating a collective movement that dismantles myths and reshapes narratives. Together, we can foster a world where every woman has the opportunity to thrive, equipped with the knowledge and confidence to navigate her financial journey.

Activity: Self-Directed Financial Learning Plan

Objective

To create a personalised learning plan for improving financial literacy and skills, allowing you to learn at your own pace.

Duration

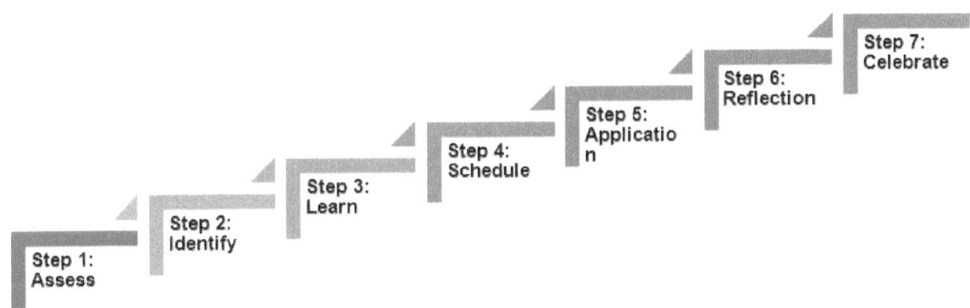

1-2 hours (initial planning) + ongoing (implementation).

Step-by-Step Guide

Step 1: Assess Your Current Knowledge

Action: Take a moment to reflect on what you already know about finances. Consider the following areas:

- Budgeting
- Saving.
- Investing.
- Debt management
- Retirement planning
- Financial products (credit cards, loans, insurance).

Tools: Use a simple checklist or write down areas where you feel confident and areas you want to improve.

Step 2: Identify Your Learning Goals

Action: Define specific financial literacy goals. Ask yourself:

- What do I want to learn? (e.g. budgeting skills, investment basics)
- Why is this important to me? (e.g. to save for a home, pay off debt)

Example Goals

- Understand how to create and stick to a monthly budget.
- Learn the basics of investing in stocks and mutual funds.
- Develop strategies for managing and reducing debt.

Step 3: Choose Your Learning Resources

Action: Research and select resources that match your goals. Consider various formats:

- **Books:** Look for recommended personal finance books.

- **Online Courses:** Platforms like Coursera, Udemy, or Khan Academy offer financial courses.

- **Podcasts/Webinars:** Find financial experts who discuss relevant topics.

- **Blogs and Websites:** Explore reputable personal finance blogs (e.g. NerdWallet, The Motley Fool).

Step 4: Create a Learning Schedule

Action: Designate specific times each week for studying. Consistency is key.

Example Schedule:

- **Monday:** 30 minutes reading a financial book.

- **Wednesday:** 1-hour online course on budgeting.

- **Friday:** Listen to a podcast episode during your commute.

Tools: Use a planner or digital calendar to set reminders.

Step 5: Engage in Practical Application

Action: Apply what you learn to your own financial situation. Consider:

- Creating a personal budget based on new insights.

- Starting a savings plan or investment account.

- Tracking expenses for a month to identify spending habits.

Tip: Document your progress in a journal to reflect on changes and challenges.

Step 6: Reflect and Adjust

Action: At the end of each month, reflect on what you've learned and how you've applied it.

- What concepts were easy to grasp?

- What areas do you still find challenging?

- Adjust your learning plan as needed based on your reflections.

Tools: Use a journal to track your thoughts and progress.

Step 7: Celebrate Milestones

Action: Acknowledge your progress, whether it's mastering a new skill or reaching a financial goal.

Tip: Treat yourself to something enjoyable (e.g., a nice meal, a day off) as a reward for your efforts.

Closing Reflection

As we conclude this Mithya, let's remember—financial literacy is not just about money; it's about empowerment, independence, and rewriting our own stories. The myths that have kept women from fully engaging with their finances are nothing more than barriers we can break. By embracing knowledge, we gain the power to shape our future, free from the limitations imposed by outdated beliefs. The journey to financial empowerment begins with a single step—learning, questioning, and taking control. Let's reclaim our narrative, one financial decision at a time.

With warm reflection,

Sakhi

Unveiling the Power Within: The Secret of SAKHI

Have you ever felt the exhilarating rush of breaking free from the chains of expectation? As we sit together at the conclusion of this journey, I reflect on the weight of the *mithyas* we've explored—each one a silent shackle that has shaped our lives in ways we often didn't recognise. From the colour pink assigned to girls to the toys that subtly enforce gender norms, from our understanding of femininity to the hushed conversations around menstruation and financial independence—these mithyas are threads woven into the very fabric of our existence.

Now, as we peel back the layers, I ask you: what have we truly learned? It's not just about tearing down these myths; it's about reclaiming the identities that have been obscured beneath them. The power of knowledge, of questioning the status quo, has been our most potent weapon. While the world may attempt to box us into narrow definitions, we've begun to write our own narratives, to find our own voices.

As I prepare to leave you, I hope you carry with you this courage—the courage to continue questioning, to delve deeper into the unseen forces that shape your life. These myths do not hold power over us anymore. We define ourselves now. Let this moment mark the beginning of your journey—one where you no longer whisper your truths but declare them boldly and confidently.

It's crucial to recognise that while these issues may appear small or even trivial, they are the roots of deeper frustrations and anger. They embed themselves in our subconscious, influencing our thoughts and behaviours. Yet, we must also understand that *Decoding MITHYAs* is not about waging war against men. The path to dismantling these myths can only be paved when we stand together, united in our quest for understanding and change.

In solidarity, we will rise. Together, we have shattered the silence. Now, we step forward—stronger, empowered, and resolute in our commitment to a future where every voice matters, including our own.

But what if I told you that the most powerful voice of all has been waiting within you?

Let me share a secret with you, I say, leaning in closer, my voice softer. Sakhi is no one but you—your inner voice, the part of you that has been submerged beneath the weight of expectations, fears, and the myths we've explored together. She represents the strength and wisdom that resides within each of us, often overshadowed by the noise of the world.

Too often, we silence this voice, allowing societal pressures to dictate our identities. But as we journey through *Decoding the 5 Mithyas*, we've uncovered the layers that obscure our true selves. It's time to reclaim that voice, to listen to the wisdom that has always been there, waiting to be heard.

So, as you move forward, remember: Sakhi is your reminder that empowerment begins from within. You have the strength to question, to challenge, and to rewrite your narrative. Embrace this journey of self-discovery, for its only by acknowledging and uplifting your inner voice that you can truly step into your power.

As we conclude, let us reflect on the timeless wisdom of the Bhagavad Gita:

"उद्धरेदात्मनाऽऽत्मानं नात्मानमवसादयेत्। आत्मैव ह्यात्मनो बन्धुरात्मैव रिपुरात्मनः॥"

(Bhagavad Gita, Chapter 6, Verse 5)

"Uddhared atmanatmanam natmanam avasadayet."

("One must elevate, not degrade, oneself.")

May this be our guiding light as we move forward, empowering ourselves and each other on this journey of self-discovery and transformation. Let us carry this message in our hearts, knowing that the power to change begins with us, and together, we will illuminate the path ahead.

9 798889 556971